STECK-VAUGHN

LEVEL

E

Language

EXERCISES

**Steck-Vaughn
Company**

A Subsidiary of National Education Corporation

Acknowledgments

Senior Editor: Diane Sharpe
Project Editor: Stephanie Muller
Product Development: The Wheetley Company, Inc.
Cover Design: Sue Heatly Design

Macmillan Publishing Company: Pronunciation Key, reprinted with permission of the publisher, from *Macmillan School Dictionary 1.* Copyright © 1990 Macmillan Publishing Company, a division of Macmillan, Inc.

LANGUAGE EXERCISES Series:

Level A/Pink	Level D/Gray	Level G/Gold
Level B/Orange	Level E/Red	Level H/Green
Level C/Violet	Level F/Blue	Review/Yellow

ISBN 0-8114-4194-6

2 3 4 5 6 7 8 9 0   HG   95 94 93 92 91 90

Table of Contents

UNIT 5 Composition

UNIT 6 Study Skills

Final Reviews

Synonyms

■ A **synonym** is a word that has the same or nearly the same meaning as one or more other words.
    EXAMPLE: help – aid – assist

A. Write one synonym for each word below. Write another synonym in a short phrase. Underline the synonym in the phrase.

1. river   stream   bubbling <u>brook</u>

2. enormous

3. vehicle

4. select

5. complete

6. small

7. permit

8. speedy

B. Circle the word or words in parentheses that are synonyms for the underlined word.

1. (task, hobby, chore)   Gina thought that her <u>job</u> was exciting.
2. (risky, simple, unsafe)   I thought that Gina's job was <u>dangerous</u>.
3. (graceful, coarse, awkward)   A <u>clumsy</u> person could not do the job.
4. (labored, spent, worked)   Gina <u>toiled</u> many long hours in practice.
5. (keep, lean, preserve)   She used a long pole to help <u>maintain</u> her balance.
6. (fence, wire, rope)   Have you guessed that Gina walked on a high <u>cable</u>?

C. Write three sentences about the circus. In each sentence, use a synonym for one of the words below. Underline the synonym.

| begin | lofty | scary |

1. _____
2. _____
3. _____

> ■ An **antonym** is a word that has the opposite meaning of another word.   EXAMPLE: hot – cold

A. Write an antonym for the underlined word in each phrase below.

1. <u>dark</u> blue _____
2. <u>busy</u> worker _____
3. <u>up</u> the hill _____
4. <u>noisy</u> play _____
5. <u>north</u> wind _____
6. <u>buy</u> a car _____
7. time of <u>day</u> _____
8. <u>bitter</u> taste _____
9. <u>come</u> now _____
10. <u>good</u> dog _____
11. <u>small</u> bird _____
12. <u>rough</u> road _____
13. <u>black</u> coat _____
14. <u>above</u> the neck _____

15. <u>frowning</u> face _____
16. <u>under</u> the bridge _____
17. <u>pretty</u> color _____
18. <u>cold</u> water _____
19. feeling <u>strong</u> _____
20. <u>wide</u> belt _____
21. <u>unhappy</u> face _____
22. <u>east</u> side _____
23. <u>cool</u> breeze _____
24. <u>stop</u> the car _____
25. <u>heavy</u> jacket _____
26. <u>long</u> story _____
27. <u>give</u> a gift _____
28. <u>difficult</u> task _____

B. Think of an antonym for the underlined word in each phrase below. Then write a sentence using the phrase with the antonym. Underline the antonym.

| <u>hard</u> question | <u>correct</u> answer | <u>old</u> soldier | <u>calm</u> sea | <u>curly</u> hair |

1. _____
2. _____
3. _____
4. _____
5. _____

Homonyms

> ■ **Homonyms** are words that are pronounced alike but are spelled differently and have different meanings.
> EXAMPLES: I'll – aisle   two – too – to

A. Write a short phrase that includes a homonym for each word below. Circle each homonym.

1. haul   long (hall)

2. road _____

3. sum _____

4. way _____

5. new _____

6. meat _____

> ■ <u>Two</u> is a number. <u>Too</u> means "also," "besides," or "more than enough." <u>To</u> means "toward." It is also used with such words as <u>be</u>, <u>sing</u>, <u>play</u>, and other action words.

B. Fill in the blanks with <u>two</u>, <u>too</u>, or <u>to</u>.

1. Eli was _____ frightened _____ utter a word.

2. He had heard the strange sound _____ times.

3. He went _____ his room upstairs, _____ steps at a time.

   But he heard it there, _____.

4. He decided _____ call his friend who lived _____ blocks away.

   It seemed the only thing _____ do!

> ■ <u>Their</u> means "belonging to them." <u>There</u> means "in that place." <u>They're</u> is a contraction of the words <u>they are</u>.

C. Underline the correct word in parentheses.

1. They are over (their, there, they're) standing in (their, there, they're) yard.

2. (Their, There, They're) waiting to go visit (their, there, they're) aunt and uncle.

3. (Their, There, They're) going to leave for (their, there, they're) vacation.

Homographs

> ■ **Homographs** are words that are spelled the same but have different meanings. They may also be pronounced differently.
> EXAMPLE: <u>desert</u> meaning "a barren, dry place" and <u>desert</u> also meaning "to abandon"

A. Read each sentence and the two meanings for the underlined word. Circle the meaning that tells how the word is used in the sentence.

1. Luis wrapped his <u>arms</u> around his father's neck.

   a. parts of the body   b. weapons for war

2. His father had taught him how to use a <u>bat</u>.

   a. a flying mammal   b. a rounded wooden club

3. Now his father was his greatest <u>fan</u>.

   a. a device to stir air   b. one devoted to another

4. Luis said, "Of all the fathers in the world, <u>mine</u> is the best!"

   a. belonging to me   b. to dig for gold

5. I <u>mean</u> to tell him exactly how I feel.

   a. unkind   b. intend

B. Write the homograph for each pair of meanings below. The first letter of each word is given for you.

1. a. sound made with fingers   b. a metal fastener   s_____

2. a. lame walk or step   b. not stiff   l_____

3. a. use oars to move a boat   b. a noisy fight   r_____

4. a. a tree covering   b. the sound a dog makes   b_____

5. a. to press flat   b. a yellow vegetable   s_____

C. Write pairs of sentences that show two different meanings for each homograph below. Use a dictionary if necessary.

1. school _____

   _____

2. pupil _____

   _____

- A **prefix** or a **suffix** added to a base word changes the meaning of the word.
   EXAMPLE: re- meaning "again" + the base word <u>do</u> = <u>redo</u> meaning "to do again"
- <u>Re-</u> means "again," <u>pre-</u> means "before," <u>mis-</u> means "wrongly" or "not," <u>-able</u> means "that can be," <u>-less</u> means "without," <u>-ness</u> means "state of being."

A. Write the word formed by each combination. Then write the definition of the new word.

1. kind + ness = _____

2. pre + date = _____

3. help + less = _____

4. re + made = _____

B. Read each sentence. Use one of the prefixes or suffixes and the base word below each blank to form a new word. Write the new word in the blank.

mis-   -ful   pre-   -less   re-   -ness

1. Terry _____ her vacation by viewing the photographs
          (lives)
she took.

2. She spends _____ hours enjoying the mountain scenery.
               (end)

3. Her favorite shot shows a mountain sunset just before

_____ settled over their campsite.
       (dark)

4. Her dad didn't see Terry's look of fright when a bear

made a _____ raid on the garbage can.
           (dawn)

5. Dad had _____ the camera directions in the dim light.
             (read)

6. He did, however, get a shot of Mama Bear's _____ cubs.
                                                      (delight)

Contractions

> ■ A **contraction** is a word formed by joining two other words. An apostrophe shows where a letter or letters have been left out.   EXAMPLES: it is = it's   we will = we'll

A. Write the contraction formed by the words.

1. who + is = _____

2. could + not = _____

3. they + have = _____

4. I + will = _____

5. does + not = _____

6. should + have = _____

7. you + would = _____

8. I + have = _____

9. that + is = _____

10. did + not = _____

11. let + us = _____

12. they + are = _____

B. Use the contractions below to complete each sentence. Write the contractions on the lines.

| can't | couldn't | he'll | I'm | it's | I've | Let's |
| She's | wasn't | What'll | What's | Where's | | |

1. It _____ quite show time.

2. José called out, "_____ Pearl?"

3. "What?" shouted Sara. "_____ not here yet?"

4. "No, and _____ looked everywhere."

5. "The show _____ go on without the star," Sara wailed.

6. Sara added, "_____ we do?"

7. "_____ ask Mr. Thompson," José suggested.

8. "Yes," said Sara, "_____ know what to do."

9. Just then a voice called, "_____ all the excitement?"

10. "Pearl, _____ you!" Sara and José exclaimed.

11. "Yes," said Pearl, "I know _____ late."

12. Pearl added, "I _____ find my costume!"

Compound Words

> ■ **Compound words** may be two words written as one, two words joined by a hyphen, or two separate words.
> EXAMPLES: sunlight   ho-hum   easy chair

A. Draw a line between the two words that form each compound word below.

1. high|way
2. old-time
3. full moon
4. snowflake
5. air-conditioner

6. fire drill
7. barefoot
8. baby sitter
9. splashdown
10. sweatshirt

11. highrise
12. earthquake
13. half-mast
14. bulldog
15. skateboard

B. Use two of the words below to form a compound word that will complete each numbered sentence. Write the word on the blank.

after	back	come	hard	hood	neighbor	noon	out	ware	yard

1. Jan and I bought a hammer and nails at a _____ store.

2. Part of the fence in our _____ was broken.

3. It took most of the _____ to repair the fence.

4. We were proud of the _____.

5. Our fence was the finest in the _____.

C. Use the second word part of each compound word to make the next compound word. Write the new word.

1. clubhouse   a building used by a club

   _____houseboat_____   a boat that people can live in

   _____boathouse_____   a house for storing boats

2. teacup   a cup for drinking tea

   _____ a cake the size of a cup

   _____ a circular walking game in which players may win a cake

A. Write <u>S</u> before each pair of synonyms. Write <u>A</u> before each pair of antonyms. Write <u>H</u> before each pair of homonyms.

1. _____ more, less

2. _____ rich, wealthy

3. _____ laugh, cry

4. _____ cent, scent

5. _____ neat, tidy

6. _____ save, spend

7. _____ late, tardy

8. _____ sew, so

9. _____ heel, heal

10. _____ join, connect

11. _____ steel, steal

12. _____ certain, sure

B. Write the correct homograph in each sentence.

1. I found my red ink _____ in the dog's _____.

2. Dropping the tennis _____ on the glass table

   made quite a _____.

3. Every time they hear the bell _____, the

   elephants form a _____.

C. Add one of the following prefixes or suffixes to each underlined word to fit the meaning. Write the new word that is formed.

| re- | pre- | mis- | -ness | -able | -less |

1. to <u>wire</u> again _____

2. without <u>hope</u> _____

3. to <u>soak</u> before _____

4. able to be <u>washed</u> _____

5. wrongly <u>shapen</u> _____

6. state of being <u>good</u> _____

D. Write the contraction or compound word that means the same thing as the underlined word or words.

| tiptop | should've | upset | she'd | playmates |

1. Tom's mother said that <u>she would</u> like his room cleaned. _____

2. She wanted it in <u>perfect</u> condition before bedtime. _____

3. Tom said that his sister's <u>friends</u> made the mess. _____

4. He thought they <u>should have</u> cleaned it up. _____

5. "They <u>tipped over</u> my box of games," Tom explained. _____

A. Read each phrase and the list of words beneath it. Write **S** before each word that is a synonym of the first word in the phrase. Write **A** before each word that is an antonym.

1. **break** a window	2. **clean** air	3. **strong** legs
_____ repair	_____ pure	_____ powerful
_____ shatter	_____ polluted	_____ sturdy
_____ mend	_____ impure	_____ weak
_____ smash	_____ fresh	_____ athletic

B. Choose a synonym or antonym from each of the three groups above. Write a sentence using each word.

1. _____

2. _____

3. _____

C. Use each pair of homonyms below in a sentence.

1. hall, haul We had to haul the piano down the hall to the music room.

2. ad, add _____

3. chilly, chili _____

4. band, banned _____

5. allowed, aloud _____

D. Write about a forest fire. Use as many of the pairs of homographs below as you can. The pairs need not be in the same sentence.

blaze, blaze   bear, bear   bark, bark   wind, wind

_____

_____

_____

_____

_____

E. Add a prefix or a suffix to each numbered word. Form a new word that means the same as the definition given. Use the new word in a sentence.

| -less | -ness | re- | pre- | -able | mis- |

1. <u>use</u>, "of no use" _That broken shoelace is useless to me._

2. <u>shy</u>, "state of being shy" _____

3. <u>pay</u>, "to pay before" _____

4. <u>write</u>, "to write again" _____

5. <u>count</u>, "to count wrongly" _____

6. <u>read</u>, "able to be read" _____

F. Below each sentence are three words. Circle the two words that can form a compound word to complete the sentence. Write the compound word.

1. The roof of the house looked silver in the _____.
   light   car   moon

2. Did you suffer _____ on your skiing trip?
   frost   crystal   bite

3. The _____ is an amazing part of the body.
   sight   ball   eye

4. The moon was at its highest point at _____.
   night   summer   mid

5. Were you able to _____ the cause of the problem?
   pin   point   ball

G. Write all the contractions you know that include each word below. Then use one of the contractions you formed in a sentence about a game you like to play.

1. will _____

   Sentence: _____

2. is _____

   Sentence: _____

3. I _____

   Sentence: _____

Recognizing Sentences

> ■ A **sentence** is a group of words that expresses a complete thought. EXAMPLE: Many readers like stories about dogs.

A. Some of the groups of words below are sentences, and some are not. Write S before each group that is a sentence.

_____ 1. One famous dog story.

_____ 2. First appeared in a well-known magazine.

_____ 3. You may have read this famous story.

_____ 4. A collie named Lassie, who was owned by a poor farmer in Yorkshire, England.

_____ 5. To make money for his family.

_____ 6. The farmer sold Lassie to a wealthy duke.

_____ 7. Lassie was loyal to her first master, however.

_____ 8. Taken hundreds of miles from Yorkshire.

_____ 9. She found her way back to her first home.

_____ 10. The story became a book and then a movie.

_____ 11. Helped two child actors on their way to stardom.

_____ 12. The real-life Lassie was a dog named Toots.

_____ 13. Toots was the companion of Eric Knight, the author of the story.

_____ 14. Lived in Yorkshire as a boy, but in the United States as an adult.

_____ 15. Knight died before his story, "Lassie Come Home," became famous.

_____ 16. Was killed in World War II.

_____ 17. Toots died on Knight's farm two years later.

B. Write a sentence about one of your favorite stories.

_____

_____

Types of Sentences

> ■ A **declarative** sentence makes a statement.
>   EXAMPLE: The telephone is ringing.
> ■ An **interrogative** sentence asks a question.
>   EXAMPLE: Where are you going?

A. Write declarative or interrogative after each sentence in the conversation below.

1. What is that you're sitting on? _____

2. It's my new skibob. _____

3. What in the world is a skibob? _____

4. It's like a bicycle with skis for wheels. _____

5. How do you make it go? _____

6. I push myself off with my short skis. _____

7. How do you stop? _____

8. At the bottom of the slope, I dig into the snow with the forklike pieces on my skis. _____

B. Pretend that you are talking to the inventor of a new way to travel over land, sea, or in the air. Write four questions you'd ask and the inventor's answers. Label each sentence D for declarative or I for interrogative.

1. _____ _____

2. _____ _____

3. _____ _____

4. _____ _____

5. _____ _____

6. _____ _____

7. _____ _____

8. _____ _____

More Types of Sentences

> ■ An **imperative** sentence expresses a command or a request.
>   EXAMPLES: Answer the telephone.   Please don't shout.
> ■ An **exclamatory** sentence expresses strong or sudden feeling.
>   EXAMPLES: What fun we had at the party!   They're off!

A. Write imperative or exclamatory after each sentence.

1. Listen to that strange noise. _____

2. What a weird sound that is! _____

3. Go see what's there. _____

4. Go yourself. _____

5. I'm too scared! _____

6. Then look out the window. _____

7. What a cute kitten that is! _____

8. What scaredy-cats we were! _____

9. Go get the kitten. _____

10. Come with me. _____

11. Oh, look! _____

12. Count the rest of the kittens in the basket. _____

13. Read the note attached to the handle. _____

14. What a surprise! _____

B. Write about a time you or someone you know was frightened by something. Use at least one exclamatory sentence and one imperative sentence.

_____

_____

_____

_____

_____

Complete Subjects and Predicates

> - Every sentence has two main parts — a **complete subject** and a **complete predicate.**
> - The complete subject includes all the words that name the person, place, or thing about which something is said.
>   EXAMPLE: **My sister Sara** plays tennis.
> - The complete predicate includes all the words that tell what the subject is or does.
>   EXAMPLE: My sister Sara **plays tennis.**

A. Write **S** before each group of words that may be used as a complete subject. Write **P** before each group of words that may be used as a complete predicate.

_____ **1.** the mayor of our town

_____ **2.** has a large town square

_____ **3.** celebrate the holidays with parades

_____ **4.** an election every four years

_____ **5.** a map with every street in town

_____ **6.** were planning to build a new swimming pool

B. Complete each sentence by writing a subject or a predicate.

1. All our town council members _____.

2. _____ met in an important meeting.

3. _____ explained the problem.

4. Every interested citizen _____.

5. Our town's first settlers _____.

6. _____ planted crops.

7. _____ has been abandoned for years.

8. _____ should be preserved.

9. Some people _____.

10. _____ will have to come to vote.

11. My entire family _____.

> ■ The **simple subject** of a sentence is the main word in the complete subject.   EXAMPLE: My parents go mushroom hunting. The words My parents make up the complete subject. The word parents is the simple subject.
> ■ If the subject is made up of just one word, that word is both the complete subject and the simple subject.
>   EXAMPLE: **I** go mushroom hunting with my parents.

A. In each sentence below, draw a line between the subject and the predicate. Underline the complete subject. Circle the simple subject.

1. Freshly-picked (morels) are delicious.

2. These mushrooms can be found only in the spring.

3. A rich soil is best for morels.

4. Grassy spots are good places to look.

5. The spring must not be dry or too cold.

6. Damp earth is a good sign that morels may be found.

7. A clear, sunny sky means good hunting.

8. We never know where we'll find morels.

9. Tall, wet grasses often hide them.

10. We must work fast.

11. These spongy little mushrooms do not last long.

12. You might like to join us sometime.

B. Write five sentences about an activity you enjoy. Draw a line between the subject and the predicate. Underline the complete subject. Circle the simple subject.

1. _____

2. _____

3. _____

4. _____

5. _____

- The **simple predicate** of a sentence is a verb within the complete predicate. The verb is an action or being word.
  EXAMPLE: Holland attracts many tourists. The words attracts many tourists make up the complete predicate. The verb attracts is the simple predicate.
- The simple predicate may be a one-word verb or a verb of more than one word.
  EXAMPLES: Joan **likes** tulips. She **is planning** a garden.

A. **In each sentence below, draw a line between the subject and the predicate. Underline the complete predicate twice. Circle the simple predicate.**

1. Many Americans visit Holland in April or May.
2. The beautiful tulip blooms reach their height of glory during these months.
3. Visitors can see flowers for miles and miles.
4. Joan is dreaming of a trip to Holland someday.
5. She has seen colorful pictures of tulips in catalogs.
6. The catalogs show tulips of all colors in full bloom.
7. Joan is anxious to see the tulips herself.
8. Passing travelers can buy large bunches of flowers.
9. Every Dutch city has flowers everywhere.
10. Flower vases can be found in the cars of some Dutch people.

B. **Add a predicate for each subject below. Circle the simple predicate.**

1. My neighbor's garden _____.

2. I _____.

3. All of the flowers _____.

C. **Write four sentences about a city or a country that you would like to visit or have visited. Draw a line between the subject and the predicate. Underline the complete predicate twice. Circle the simple predicate.**

1. _____

2. _____

3. _____

4. _____

Understood Subjects

> ■ The subject of an imperative sentence is always the person to whom the command or request is given **(You).** The subject does not appear in the sentence. Therefore, it is called an **understood subject.** EXAMPLES: **(You)** Keep off the grass. **(You)** Close the door, please.

A. On the line after each imperative sentence below, write the understood subject and the simple predicate.

1. Open your books to page 23, please. _____(You) Open_____

2. Read the directions carefully. _____

3. Raise your hand if you have a question. _____

4. Make your handwriting easy to read, please. _____

5. Stand with your toes on the line. _____

6. Count off by fours. _____

7. Form relay lines by groups of four. _____

8. Run to the opposite wall and back. _____

9. Wait! _____

10. Shake the snow off your boots before you come in. _____

11. Hang your wet gloves, hats, and jackets on the hooks by the back door. _____

12. Come into the kitchen for some hot chocolate. _____

B. Write four imperative sentences about a game or other activity. After each sentence, write the understood subject.

1. _____

2. _____

3. _____

4. _____

> ■ Two sentences that have different subjects but the same predicate can be combined to make one sentence. The two subjects are joined by <u>and</u>. The subject of the new sentence is called a **compound subject.**   EXAMPLE: **Craig** likes tall tales. **Jack** likes tall tales. **Craig and Jack** like tall tales.

A. In each sentence below, underline the subject. If the subject is compound, write C before the sentence.

_____ **1.** Paul Bunyan and Babe were the subject of many tall tales.

_____ **2.** Babe was Paul's blue ox.

_____ **3.** Maine and Minnesota are two of the states that have tall tales about Paul and Babe.

_____ **4.** Babe could haul the timber from 640 acres at one time.

_____ **5.** Lumberjacks and storytellers liked to tell tall tales about Paul and Babe's great deeds.

B. Combine each pair of sentences below to make a sentence that has a compound subject. Underline the compound subject.

1. Tennessee claims Davy Crockett as its hero. Texas claims Davy Crockett as its hero.

_____

2. Great bravery made Davy Crockett famous. Unusual skills made Davy Crockett famous.

_____

3. True stories about Davy Crockett were passed down. Tall tales about Davy Crockett were passed down.

_____

4. These true stories made Davy Crockett a legend. These tall tales made Davy Crockett a legend.

_____

C. Write a sentence using <u>Paul Bunyan and Davy Crockett</u> as the subject.

_____

_____

Using Compound Predicates

> ■ Two sentences that have the same subject but different predicates can be combined to make one sentence. The two predicates may be joined by <u>or</u>, <u>and</u>, or <u>but</u>. The predicate of the sentence is called a **compound predicate.**
> EXAMPLE: A newspaper **informs its readers.** A newspaper **entertains its readers.** A newspaper **informs and entertains its readers.**

A. In each sentence below, underline the predicate. If the predicate is compound, write <u>C</u> before the sentence.

_____ 1. Mrs. Oliver's class wrote and printed its own newspaper.

_____ 2. Leslie was named editor-in-chief.

_____ 3. She assigned the stories and approved the final copies.

_____ 4. Wong and several other students were reporters.

_____ 5. They either wrote the news stories or edited the stories.

_____ 6. Wong interviewed a new student and wrote up the interview.

B. Combine each pair of sentences below to make a sentence that has a compound predicate. Underline the compound predicate.

1. Jenny covered the baseball game. Jenny described the best plays.

_____

2. Sue and Kim wrote jokes. Sue and Kim made up puzzles.

_____

3. Luis corrected the news stories. Luis wrote headlines.

_____

4. Mrs. Oliver typed the newspaper.
   Mrs. Oliver couldn't print the newspaper.

_____

C. Pretend that you are Wong or Jenny. Write a sentence that has a compound predicate which could begin the story on the baseball game.

_____

Simple and Compound Sentences

- A **simple sentence** has one subject and one predicate.
  EXAMPLE: Our country's presidents/led interesting lives.
- A **compound sentence** is made up of two simple sentences joined by connecting words such as and, but, and or. A comma is placed before the connecting word.
  EXAMPLE: George Washington led the army in the Revolutionary War, **and** Ulysses S. Grant led it in the Civil War.

A. Draw a line between each subject and predicate. Write S before each simple sentence. Write C before each compound sentence.

_____ 1. George Washington witnessed the first successful balloon flight.

_____ 2. John Adams was our second president, and his son was our sixth.

_____ 3. Thomas Jefferson was very interested in experiments with balloons and submarines.

_____ 4. The British burned the White House in 1814, but President Madison escaped unharmed.

B. Combine each pair of simple sentences below into a compound sentence.

1. Andrew Jackson was called "Old Hickory."
   Zachary Taylor's nickname was "Old Rough and Ready."

   _____

   _____

2. Four presidents had no children. John Tyler had fourteen children.

   _____

   _____

3. Chester A. Arthur put the first bathroom in the White House. Benjamin Harrison put in electric lights.

   _____

   _____

4. Woodrow Wilson coached college football. Ronald Reagan announced baseball games on radio.

   _____

   _____

Correcting Run-on Sentences

> ■ Two or more sentences that are run together without the correct punctuation are called a **run-on sentence.**
>   EXAMPLE: Animals that carry their young in the mother's pouch are called marsupials, they live mainly in Australia.
> ■ Correct a run-on sentence by making separate sentences from its parts.
>   EXAMPLE: Animals that carry their young in the mother's pouch are called marsupials. They live mainly in Australia.

A. **Separate the run-on sentences below. Write the last word of the first sentence. Place a period after the word. Then write the first word of the second sentence. Be sure to capitalize the word. One run-on sentence is made of three sentences.**

1. There are over two hundred kinds of marsupials all live in North or South America or in Australia.

   1. _____ marsupials. _____
      _____ All _____

2. The kangaroo is the largest marsupial, the male red kangaroo may be up to seven feet tall.

   2. _____
      _____

3. Wallabies are similar to kangaroos, they are smaller than kangaroos, some are the size of a rabbit.

   3. _____
      _____
      _____
      _____

4. Kangaroos and wallabies live only in Australia, their hind feet are larger than their front feet.

   4. _____
      _____

B. **Correct the run-on sentences in the paragraph below. Use the proofreader's symbols as shown in parentheses. (The opossum is active at night, it plays dead if frightened.) There will be seven sentences.**

Opossums are the only marsupials that live north of Mexico, they also live in Central and South America. Opossums are grayish white, they have a long snout, hairless ears, and a long, hairless tail. Opossums have fifty teeth, the opossum mother has from five to twenty babies, each baby is the size of a kidney bean.

A. Label each sentence as follows: Write D in front of each declarative sentence. Write IN in front of each interrogative sentence. Write IM in front of each imperative sentence. Write E in front of each exclamatory sentence. Write X if the group of words is not a sentence.

_____ 1. Did you know that the first bicycle had no pedals?

_____ 2. Very tiring and could not be steered.

_____ 3. The rider pushed himself forward by walking.

_____ 4. Made the first bicycle with pedals in Scotland.

_____ 5. What a great improvement it was!

_____ 6. What did the public think of this bicycle?

_____ 7. Get that machine off the road.

_____ 8. Say today about bicycles?

B. In each sentence below, draw a line between the complete subject and the complete predicate. Underline the simple subject once. Underline the simple predicate twice. One sentence has an understood subject. Write the understood subject on the line after that sentence.

1. The next bicycle was known as the "boneshaker." _____

2. Its wheels were made of wood. _____

3. A new feature was tires made of iron. _____

4. Guess how this bicycle got its name. _____

C. Label the sentences below as follows: CS if the sentence has a compound subject; CP if the sentence has a compound predicate; CSt if the sentence is compound; and RS if the sentence is run-on.

_____ 1. Wire-spoked wheels and rubber tires came next.

_____ 2. Gradually the front wheel became larger, the rear wheel became smaller.

_____ 3. Wooden parts were done away with, and iron was used instead.

_____ 4. An air-filled rubber tire brought comfort and attracted more cyclists.

A. Two of the groups of words below are sentences, and three are not. Write <u>S</u> before each sentence. Add whatever is needed to the groups of words to make them complete sentences.

_____ **1.** The minute Scott heard his name called. _____

_____ **2.** Amy was sure that her name would be called next. _____

_____ **3.** The feeling of nervousness was mounting. _____

_____ **4.** Only three possible names. _____

_____ **5.** Amy could hardly. _____

B. Complete each sentence below to make the kind of sentence named.

Declarative   **1.** An expert is one who _____.

Interrogative   **2.** Why did the expert _____.

Imperative   **3.** Read the _____.

Exclamatory   **4.** What a perfect _____.

C. Add to each subject or predicate below whatever is needed to make a sentence. Underline the simple subject once and the simple predicate twice.

1. The dangerous tornado _____.

2. A raging wind storm _____.

3. _____ had flooded the downtown area.

4. Homeowners for several blocks _____.

5. _____ created puddles two feet deep.

6. _____ rescued a helpless motorist.

D. Write three sentences in which <u>You</u> is the understood subject. Include one of the verbs below in each sentence.

hide	do	think	give	walk	sit

1. _____

2. _____

3. _____

E. Write a compound subject for each predicate. Underline the simple predicate twice.

1. _____ opened the special event.

2. _____ were given to our school.

3. _____ presented the awards.

4. _____ received a lot of praise.

F. Write a compound predicate for each subject. Underline the simple subject.

1. The bank robber _____.

2. The undercover detective _____.

3. One innocent bystander _____.

4. The trembling bank clerk _____.

G. Rewrite the sentences below by making one of these improvements: (a) combine sentences by using compound subjects or compound predicates; (b) combine simple sentences to make compound sentences; (c) correct run-on sentences.

1. Marcella Gruell was playing in the attic, she found an old doll.

   _____

2. Her dad gave the doll a new face. He added button eyes.

   _____

3. One friend wrote a poem about Raggedy Ann. Another friend made a twin doll.

   _____

4. The twin was a boy, Marcella named it Andy.

   _____

5. Raggedy Ann became famous in the stories Marcella's dad wrote. Raggedy Andy became famous in those same stories.

   _____

6. John Gruell was a well-known cartoonist. James Whitcomb Riley was a famous poet.

   _____

   _____

> ■ A **noun** is a word that names a person, place, thing, or quality. EXAMPLES: Rachel, Chad, city, Montana, shell, animal, love, freedom, happiness

A. Write nouns that name the following:

1. Four people you admire

_____   _____

_____   _____

2. Four places you would like to visit

_____   _____

_____   _____

3. Six things you use every day

_____   _____

_____   _____

_____   _____

4. Four qualities you would like to have

_____   _____

_____   _____

5. Four states in the United States

_____   _____

_____   _____

B. Find and underline twenty-six nouns in the sentences below.

1. Every section of the United States has scenes of natural beauty.

2. The tall trees in California are called the giants of the forest.

3. Every fall, tourists go to see the colorful trees in Vermont.

4. Southern coastal cities are proud of their sandy beaches.

5. Colorful flowers and grasses cover the prairies of Texas.

6. Montana and Wyoming boast of majestic mountains.

7. The citizens of every state take pride in the charm of their own state.

Common and Proper Nouns

- There are two main classes of nouns: **common** and **proper nouns.**
- A **common noun** is a word that names any one of a class of objects.   EXAMPLES: girl, city, dog
- A **proper noun** is the name of a particular person, place, or thing. It begins with a capital letter.
  EXAMPLES: Sue, Nashville, Digger

A. Write a proper noun for each common noun below.

1. city _____
2. school _____
3. friend _____
4. ocean _____
5. state _____
6. car _____
7. singer _____
8. day _____
9. lake _____

10. street _____
11. game _____
12. river _____
13. woman _____
14. country _____
15. man _____
16. president _____
17. month _____
18. planet _____

B. Write a common noun for each proper noun below.

1. Alaska _____
2. November _____
3. Thanksgiving _____
4. Betsy _____
5. December _____
6. Hawaii _____
7. *Call of the Wild* _____
8. Saturday _____
9. *The Cosby Show* _____

10. South America _____
11. Dr. Cooke _____
12. Rocky Mountains _____
13. Abraham Lincoln _____
14. Sahara _____
15. Denver _____
16. Mexico _____
17. Saturn _____
18. Jason _____

Singular and Plural Nouns

21

> - A **singular noun** is a noun that names one person, place, or thing.   EXAMPLES: knife, church, boy, mouse
> - A **plural noun** is a noun that names more than one person, place, or thing.   EXAMPLES: knives, churches, boys, mice

A. Write S before each singular noun below. Then write its plural form. Write P before each plural noun. Then write its singular form. You may wish to check the spellings in a dictionary.

_____ 1. boots _____

_____ 2. army _____

_____ 3. match _____

_____ 4. maps _____

_____ 5. inches _____

_____ 6. foot _____

_____ 7. hero _____

_____ 8. alley _____

_____ 9. lady _____

_____ 10. women _____

_____ 11. halves _____

_____ 12. skies _____

_____ 13. wife _____

_____ 14. boxes _____

_____ 15. beach _____

_____ 16. book _____

B. Write the plural form of each word below to complete the sentences.

watch	shelf	child	story	monkey	player

1. There are many interesting _____ in that magazine.

2. The cover story on timepieces describes the making of _____.

3. A sports story contains conversations with three of the nation's leading

   football _____.

4. A do-it-yourself article shows how to build _____ that will hold an aquarium.

5. Unusual _____ and apes are shown in a picture story.

6. This month's special article is a selection of poems and stories by

   German _____.

Singular Possessive Nouns

> - A **possessive noun** shows possession of the noun that follows.   EXAMPLES: mother's car, the dog's bone
> - To form the possessive of most singular nouns, add an apostrophe (') and -s.   EXAMPLES: Sally's room, the city's mayor

A. Write the possessive form of the noun in parentheses to complete each phrase.

1. the _____ leash   (dog)

2. the _____ lawn   (neighbor)

3. one of the _____ engines   (plane)

4. _____ greatest ambition   (Ann)

5. to _____ house   (grandmother)

6. the _____ paw   (tiger)

7. my _____ farm   (uncle)

8. your _____ best friend   (brother)

9. our _____ advice   (mother)

10. your _____ gym   (school)

11. my _____ apple   (teacher)

12. that _____ fur   (cat)

13. the _____ teeth   (dinosaur)

14. the _____ coach   (team)

B. Write each of the phrases below in a shorter way.

1. the friend of Aunt Amanda   Aunt Amanda's friend

2. the car of the friend   _____

3. the keeper of the zoo   _____

4. the roar of the lion   _____

5. the cage of the tiger   _____

Unit 3, Grammar and Usage

Plural Possessive Nouns

23

- To form the possessive of a plural noun ending in -s, add only an apostrophe.
    EXAMPLES: the boys' coats, the books' covers
- To form the possessive of a plural noun that does not end in -s, add an apostrophe and -s.
    EXAMPLES: men's suits, children's toys

A. Complete the chart below. You may wish to check the spellings in a dictionary.

Singular noun	Plural noun	Singular possessive	Plural possessive
1. boy	boys	boy's	boys'
2. bird			
3. teacher			
4. child			
5. truck			
6. doctor			
7. man			
8. church			

B. Rewrite each sentence using a possessive noun.

1. The cat of the Smiths has three kittens.

   _____

2. The names of the kittens are Frisky, Midnight, and Puff.

   _____

3. The dogs of the neighbors are very playful.

   _____

4. The pen of the dogs is in the yard.

   _____

5. The curiosity of the cats might get them into trouble.

   _____

> - A **verb** is a word that shows action. The verb may show
>   action that can be seen.
>   EXAMPLE: Jane **opened** the door.
> - The verb may show action that cannot be seen.
>   EXAMPLE: May **thought** about it.

A. Underline the verb in each sentence.

1. Our school <u>holds</u> a field day every year.
2. Each student enters two events.
3. Last year Mel won both his events.
4. He ran the two-mile race the fastest ever.
5. He also jumped higher than anyone else.
6. Marie finished second in the high jump.
7. Andy beat her by less than an inch.
8. Then Andy lost to Betty in the fifty-yard dash.
9. Betty usually wins that race each year.
10. Our class won the relay race.
11. We ran it in record time.
12. Our principal shook hands with the winners.

B. Complete each sentence with one of the verbs below.
Use each verb once.

believe	felt	hoped	knew	remember	studied	thought	worried

1. Yoko really _____ about the math test.
2. She _____ every day after school.
3. She _____ she could pass the test.
4. During the test, Yoko _____ carefully about each problem.
5. Could she _____ all she had studied?
6. She _____ more confident once the test was over.
7. She _____ that she had done well.
8. When Yoko got her test back, she couldn't _____ she got an A!

Helping Verbs

> ■ A verb may have a **main verb** and one or more **helping verbs.**
> Such a verb is called a **verb phrase.** Where **have** you
> EXAMPLES: The bells **were ringing.** Where **have** you
> **been hiding?**

A. Underline each main verb. Circle each helping verb. Some verbs do not have a helping verb.

1. (Have) you heard of Casey Jones?

2. He was born John Luther Jones in Cayce (Kay' see), Kentucky.

3. As a railroad engineer, he could make sad music with
   his locomotive whistle.

4. Soon people were telling stories about Casey.

5. One of the stories was about his train wreck.

6. One day he had climbed into his engine cab.

7. The train was carrying the mail.

8. It had been pouring rain for more than a week.

9. The railroad track was covered with water.

10. They were running late.

11. But maybe they could make it on time!

12. Around a curve, they saw a passenger train.

13. Everyone jumped.

14. But Casey did his job, faithful and true to the end.

15. People still sing about this brave railroad man.

B. Complete each sentence by adding <u>have</u>, <u>will</u>, or <u>would</u>.

1. Marla and Ricardo _____ like to go swimming.

2. They _____ received permission from their parents.

3. This _____ be their second trip to the pool today.

Present and Past Tense

> - A verb in the **present tense** shows an action that happens now.   EXAMPLE: I **watch** TV.
> - A verb in the **past tense** shows an action that happened in the past.   EXAMPLE: I **watched** TV.

A. Underline each verb in the present tense.

1. A famous poem tells about another Casey.
2. This Casey plays baseball.
3. His great skill with the bat makes him a hero.
4. The people in the town of Mudville call him the Mighty Casey.
5. Casey is one of the greatest players.
6. He frightens pitchers.
7. He often hits the winning run for his team.
8. The fans love Casey.

B. Underline each verb or verb phrase in the past tense.

1. The game had reached the last inning.
2. The Mudville team trailed four to two.
3. The first two batters were called out at first base.
4. Many in the crowd left the game and went home.
5. But the next two men up made hits.
6. Then Casey came up to the plate.
7. The crowd went wild.

C. List four verbs you know.

	present tense	past tense
1.		
2.		
3.		
4.		

Future Tense

> ■ A verb in the **future tense** shows an action that will happen
> at some time in the future. The helping verb <u>will</u> is used
> with the present tense form of the verb.
> EXAMPLE: I **will meet** you tomorrow.

A. Write a verb in the future tense to complete each sentence.

1. Sue _____ the invitations.

2. David and Andrew _____ what games to play.

3. We all _____ the balloons with air.

4. Mary and Ella _____ the table decorations.

5. Carlos and Rosa _____ the cake.

6. Chris _____ of a way to get Tony to come over.

7. We all _____ in the back room.

8. When Chris and Tony come in, everyone _____, "Surprise!"

**B. The sentences below show an event that happened in the past. Rewrite
each underlined verb to change the event to a time in the future.**

1. Fran <u>sent</u> a letter to the Round-the-World Travel Agency.   _____ will send _____

2. She <u>received</u> an answer in a day or two.   _____

3. The agency <u>mailed</u> her folders containing information
   about exciting places to visit.   _____

4. Fran <u>studied</u> the information.   _____

5. She <u>chose</u> to write about three places.   _____

6. Then she <u>planned</u> an imaginary trip to those three
   places.   _____

7. She <u>wrote</u> in detail about her imaginary trip.   _____

8. She <u>designed</u> her report with pictures from the
   travel agency folders.   _____

9. She <u>made</u> an interesting cover for her report.   _____

10. Then she <u>hoped</u> for a good grade.   _____

> - A **singular subject** must have a **singular verb**.
>   EXAMPLES: Jane **lives** there. She **does walk** to school.
>   She **doesn't live** near me.
> - A **plural subject** must have a **plural verb**.
>   EXAMPLES: Jane and her sister **live** there. They **do walk**
>   to school. They **don't live** near me.
> - You and I must have a plural verb.

- **Write S over each singular subject. Write P over each plural subject.
  Then underline the correct verb in parentheses.**

1. Many stories (tell, tells) how dogs become friends of people.

2. A story by Rudyard Kipling (say, says) that Wild Dog
   agreed to help hunt and guard in exchange for bones.

3. After that, Wild Dog (become, becomes) First Friend.

4. Many dogs never (leave, leaves) their masters.

5. In another story, a dog (doesn't, don't) leave his master's
   dead body and dies in the Arctic cold.

6. There are few people in history that (doesn't, don't)
   record the usefulness of dogs.

7. Diggings in Egypt (prove, proves) that the dog was a
   companion in ancient Egypt.

8. Bones of dogs (does, do) appear in Egyptian graves.

9. Ancient Greek vases (picture, pictures) dogs on them.

10. Today the Leader Dog organization (train, trains) dogs
    to guide the blind.

11. One blind man said, "My eyes (have, has) a wet nose."

12. A dog (does, do) have excellent hearing and smelling abilities.

13. What person (doesn't, don't) agree that a dog is a
    person's best friend?

> - A **linking verb** is a verb that joins the subject of a sentence with a word in the predicate.
>   EXAMPLES: Bob **is** an artist. Bob **was** late.
> - A singular subject must have a singular linking verb.
>   EXAMPLES: Maria **is** a singer. Maria **was** happy.
> - A plural subject must have a plural linking verb.
>   EXAMPLES: Becky and Lynn **are** sisters. The sisters **were** pretty.
> - You must have a plural linking verb.

A. Write S over each singular subject. Write P over each plural subject. Then circle the correct linking verb.

1. Tracy (is, are) a clown.

2. Her brothers (is, are) acrobats.

3. Tracy and her brothers (was, were) in a show.

4. Tracy (was, were) funny.

5. Her brothers (was, were) daring.

6. The people watching (was, were) delighted.

7. Tracy (was, were) amusing with her big red nose.

8. Tracy's brothers (was, were) high in the air on a swing.

9. (Was, Were) you ever at their show?

10. Tracy (is, are) glad that I went to see her perform.

B. Circle the correct linking verb in parentheses.
1. Ice skating (is, are) a popular winter sport today.
2. (Isn't, Aren't) there a skating rink or pond in every northern town?
3. Even in many southern towns, there (is, are) an indoor rink.
4. The discovery of ice skating (were, was) an accident.
5. An Arctic settler who slipped on a piece of bone and skidded across the ice (was, were) the inventor of the ice skate.
6. Pieces of bone attached to his feet (was, were) the first ice skates.
7. Now we (is, are) all able to enjoy his invention.
8. That (was, were) a lucky day for all ice skaters!

Forms of *Go, Do, See,* and *Sing*

30

> - Never use a helping verb with <u>went</u>, <u>did</u>, <u>saw</u>, or <u>sang</u>.
>   EXAMPLES: Sue **did** her work. Sam **went** home. Sarah **sang** a song.
> - Always use a helping verb with <u>gone</u>, <u>done</u>, <u>seen</u>, or <u>sung</u>.
>   EXAMPLES: Sarah **has done** her work. Mary **had** not **seen** me.

A. Circle the correct verb in parentheses.

1. Miss Taylor's class (did, done) very well on their music project.
2. Most of the class members had (gone, went) to extra practices.
3. They (sang, sung) at the special spring concert.
4. The class had (sang, sung) in the concert before, but they (did, done) even better this year.
5. Miss Taylor said she had never (saw, seen) a class work so well together.
6. Miss Taylor said they had (sang, sung) beautifully.
7. They (sang, sung) so well that she was very proud of them.
8. The week after the concert, the class (gone, went) to a music museum.
9. The trip was a reward because the class had (did, done) so well.
10. The class (saw, seen) pictures of famous musicians at the museum.
11. After they had (saw, seen) an exhibit of unusual music boxes, they wished the boxes were for sale.
12. What do you think Miss Taylor (did, done)?
13. She took the class to a music shop she had (gone, went) to before.
14. Miss Taylor and the shop owner had (sang, sung) together.
15. They had (gone, went) to the same music school.
16. So the class (went, gone) to this shop and saw many little musical toys.
17. In the shop they (saw, seen) many small music boxes.

B. Write the correct form of each verb in parentheses.

1. (go) Katie has _____ away to summer camp.
2. (sing) She and her friend Tanya have _____ campfire songs together.
3. (do) Her other friends have _____ different things.
4. (see) All of the children have _____ wild animals at camp.

> - Never use a helping verb with <u>broke</u>, <u>drank</u>, <u>took</u>, or <u>wrote</u>.
>   EXAMPLES: Kim **broke** her arm. Mother **wrote** a letter.
> - Always use a helping verb with <u>broken</u>, <u>drunk</u>, <u>taken</u>, or <u>written</u>.
>   EXAMPLES: Kim **has broken** her arm. Mom **had written** a note.

A. Complete each sentence with the correct form of one of the verbs below.

| broke, broken | drank, drunk | took, taken | wrote, written |

1. Little Rachel always _____ from her Minnie Mouse mug.

2. She got it when her parents _____ the family to Florida.

3. She had _____ her milk from it every day for two years.

4. One morning Rachel dropped the mug, and it _____.

5. She cried as if her heart had been _____, too.

6. Her big brother Jim said, "If I _____ a letter
   to Minnie, she'd send you another."

7. So Jim _____ a letter to Aunt Minnie in Florida.

8. When the new mug arrived in a few days, Rachel couldn't

   believe it hadn't _____ longer.

9. Jim just smiled because he knew Rachel thought he had

   _____ to Minnie Mouse.

10. That was two years ago, and the mug hasn't been _____ yet.

B. Write the correct form of each verb in parentheses.

1. (take)   Al had _____ his dog for a long walk and was thirsty.

2. (drink)   So he had _____ a glass of fruit juice.

3. (break)   He was careful and had not _____ the glass.

4. (break)   But then his dog, Ruby, had _____ it.

5. (write)   Now Al has _____ a note of apology to his mom.

Forms of *Eat, Draw, Give,* and *Ring*

- Never use a helping verb with <u>ate</u>, <u>drew</u>, <u>gave</u>, or <u>rang</u>.
  EXAMPLES: Ann **ate** her lunch. The telephone **rang**.
- Always use a helping verb with <u>eaten</u>, <u>drawn</u>, <u>given</u>, or <u>rung</u>.
  EXAMPLES: Ann **has eaten** her lunch. The telephone
  has rung.

A. Complete each sentence with the correct form of the verb in parentheses.

1. (give) Martha _____ samples of the granola bars she had made to
   three of her friends.

2. (eat) The bars were soon _____, and there were cries of "More!"

3. (eat) "You _____ those already?" Martha asked.

4. (give) "I should have _____ you the recipe."

5. (eat) "Please do!" said her friends. "We have never _____
   anything so delicious."

6. (give) "I _____ them to you for your health's sake," said Martha.

7. (ring) Just then the school bell _____.

8. (ring) "Someone must have _____ the bell too soon," Paul said.

9. (draw) "No, it's time for art class," said Martha. "Have you
   _____ your design yet?"

10. (draw) "I _____ something yesterday, but I wasn't happy with it."

11. (draw) "Oh, but you have _____ some beautiful designs before,"
    Martha said.

B. Circle the correct verb in parentheses.

1. The telephone has just (rang, rung).

2. Carla and Betty have (drew, drawn) pictures all morning and
   are looking for something else to do.

3. Now Joseph has (gave, given) them a call to ask if they
   would like to come to his house.

Unit 3, Grammar and Usage

Forms of *Begin, Fall, Steal,* and *Throw*

33

- Never use a helping verb with <u>began</u>, <u>fell</u>, <u>stole</u>, or <u>threw</u>.
  EXAMPLES: Sue **began** to run. Freddie **fell** down.
- Always use a helping verb with <u>begun</u>, <u>fallen</u>, <u>stolen</u>, or <u>thrown</u>.
  EXAMPLES: Sue **had begun** to run. Freddie **had fallen**.

A. Circle the correct verb in parentheses.

1. Spring baseball practice had just (began, begun).

2. The pitchers on the Blasters' team had (threw, thrown) a few balls.

3. The other Blasters (began, begun) to practice.

4. They would need lots of practice, because they had (fell, fallen) into last place at the end of last season.

5. The Blasters' coaches (threw, thrown) themselves into their work.

6. The biggest job (fell, fallen) on the batting and base-running coach.

7. The team batting average had (fell, fallen) out of sight.

8. And the players had (stole, stolen) only forty bases last year.

9. The coach said, "Our team motto will be 'We have just (began, begun) to fight!' "

10. With that, the Blasters (fell, fallen) to work.

11. The pitchers (threw, thrown) many different kinds of pitches.

12. The fastest pitch was (threw, thrown) at ninety miles per hour.

13. The batters were hitting everything that was (threw, thrown) to them.

B. Write the correct form of each verb in parentheses.

1. (steal)   In last night's opening game, Nick, our team's fastest

   base runner, had _____ home.

2. (begin)   We had _____ to warm up Willis, our relief pitcher,

   before the sixth inning.

3. (throw)   He had _____ the ball so well last year that

   no batters could hit his pitches.

4. (begin)   After Willis won last night's game for us, we told him that

   he had _____ our season in great style.

Subject and Object Pronouns

34

- A **pronoun** is a word that is used in place of a noun.
  EXAMPLES: Dick read a story. **He** enjoyed the story.
- A **subject pronoun** is a pronoun that is used as the subject of a sentence. He, I, it, she, they, we, and you are subject pronouns.
  EXAMPLES: **She** helped Dad. **I** helped, too.
- An **object pronoun** is a pronoun that is used in place of a noun that receives the action of the verb. Her, him, it, me, them, us, and you are object pronouns.
  EXAMPLES: Diane called **me**. I answered **her**.

A. Circle the subject pronoun that could be used in place of the underlined subject.

1. Susan (Her, She) saw the bus nearing the corner.
2. Mr. Hanes (Him, He) ran down the driveway to stop the bus.
3. The children (Them, They) saw Susan from the bus windows.
4. Ann (Her, She) called to Mrs. Thomas, the driver, to wait.
5. The bus (It, He) stopped just in time.
6. Mrs. Thomas (Her, She) let Susan on the bus.
7. Then Susan (her, she) waved goodbye to Mr. Hanes.
8. Susan (Her, She) was glad the bus waited for her.

B. Circle the correct object pronoun that could be used in place of the underlined object.

1. "Tony invited Bill and (I, me) to his birthday party," said Tom.
2. "He asked Tom and Bill (us, we) to be right on time," Bill said.
3. "Tony's parents are giving Tony (he, him) a special treat," Tom said. "They are giving him tickets to the baseball game."
4. "They bought the tickets (them, they) last week."
5. Bill asked, "Do you think Tony's mother bought Tony Bill, and Tom (us, we) front row seats?"
6. "Let's ask Tony's mother (her, she)," Tom answered.

> - A **possessive pronoun** is a pronoun that shows who or what owns something.
>   EXAMPLES: The shoes are **mine.** Those are **my** shoes.
> - The possessive pronouns <u>hers</u>, <u>mine</u>, <u>ours</u>, <u>theirs</u>, and <u>yours</u> stand alone.
>   EXAMPLES: The dog is **mine.** This book is **yours.**
> - The possessive pronouns <u>her</u>, <u>its</u>, <u>my</u>, <u>our</u>, <u>their</u>, and <u>your</u> must be used before nouns.
>   EXAMPLES: **Their** house is gray. **Her** cat is white.
> - The pronoun <u>his</u> may be used either way.
>   EXAMPLES: That is **his** bike. The bike is **his.**

A. Circle the possessive pronoun that completes each sentence.

1. Carol lent me (her, hers) sweater.

2. I thought that (her, hers) was warmer than mine.

3. We often trade (our, ours) jackets and sweaters.

4. My mom says I'll soon forget which are (her, hers) and which are (my, mine).

5. My cousin Jane and I have the same problem with (our, ours) bikes.

6. Both of (our, ours) are the same make and model.

7. The only difference is that (mine, my) handlebar grips are blue and (her, hers) are pink.

8. What kind of dog is (your, yours)?

9. (Your, Yours) dog's ears are pointed.

10. (It, Its) tail is stubby.

B. Complete each pair of sentences by writing the correct possessive pronoun.

1. Bill owns a beautiful horse named Tony.

   _____ spots are brown and white.

2. Bill has taught the horse some tricks.

   In fact, _____ horse counts with its hoof.

3. Bill's sisters have horses, too.

   Bill is going to train them for _____ sisters.

> ■ An **adjective** is a word that describes a noun or a pronoun.
>   EXAMPLE: The field is dotted with **beautiful** flowers.
> ■ Adjectives usually tell **what kind, which one,** or **how many.**
>   EXAMPLES: **tall** trees, the **other** hat, **five** dollars

A. In the sentences below, underline each adjective and circle the noun it describes. Some sentences may contain more than one adjective. Do not include a, an, or the.

1. The early Greeks admired a healthy body.

2. They believed that strong bodies meant healthy minds.

3. The Olympics began in Greece in the distant past.

4. The great god Zeus and the powerful Cronus both wanted to own Earth.

5. They battled on the high peaks of the beautiful mountains of Greece.

6. Zeus won the mighty struggle, and the first Olympics were
   held in the peaceful valley below Mount Olympus.

B. Expand the meaning of each sentence below by writing an adjective to describe each underlined noun.

1. The _____ runners from _____ nations lined up
   for the race.

2. Several _____ skaters competed for the _____ medal.

3. The _____ skiers sped down the _____ slopes.

4. We noticed the _____ colors of their _____ clothing

   against the _____ snow.

5. Hundreds of _____ fans greeted the _____ winners
   of each event.

6. As the _____ national song of the winner's country

   was played, _____ tears streamed down her _____ face.

C. Fill in each blank with an adjective telling how many or which one.

1. _____ days of vacation   3. the _____ row of desks

2. the _____ race   4. _____ library books

Adjectives That Compare

> ■ Adjectives that compare two nouns end in -er.
>   EXAMPLES: Jack is **taller** than Bill. Bill is **heavier** than Jack.
> ■ Adjectives that compare more than two nouns end in -est.
>   EXAMPLE: Sam is the **tallest** and **heaviest** in the class.
> ■ Most longer adjectives use more and most to compare.
>   EXAMPLES: **more** beautiful, **most** beautiful

■ **Underline the correct form of the adjective.**

1. Last year's science fair was the (bigger, biggest) one our school has ever had.

2. For one thing, it had the (larger, largest) attendance ever.

3. Also, most students felt that the projects were (more interesting, most interesting) than last year's.

4. Of the two models of the solar system, Ray's was the (larger, largest).

5. However, Mary's model was (more accurate, most accurate) in scale.

6. The judges had a difficult task, but they gave the (higher, highest) rating to Mary's model.

7. Sue's, Tim's, and Becky's projects on cameras drew the (bigger, biggest) crowds at the fair.

8. These projects were the (more popular, most popular) of all.

9. Sue's project had the (prettier, prettiest) display of photographs.

10. But Becky's showed the (greater, greatest) understanding of a camera's workings.

11. Tim's project, however, was the (finer, finest) all-around project of the three.

12. One judge said, "This was the (harder, hardest) job I've ever had."

> ■ An **adverb** is a word that describes a verb. It tells **how, when, where,** or **how often** the action shown by a verb happens.
> ■ Many adverbs end in -ly.
>   EXAMPLES: The bell rang **loudly.** The bell rang **today.**
>   The bell rang **downstairs.** The bell rang **often.**

A. Circle each verb. Then underline each adverb that describes the verb. Next, write how, when, where, or how often.

1. The boys had talked daily about visiting the empty old house. _____ when _____

2. They often walked by it on their way to school. _____

3. But they seldom had time to stop. _____

4. They suddenly decided that today was the day. _____

5. So on the way home from school, they slipped quietly through the front gate. _____

6. They crept carefully up the creaky front steps. _____

7. Rob quietly opened the front door. _____

8. Dick then peered into the darkness of the front hall. _____

9. A draft of wind instantly swept through the house. _____

10. The back door banged loudly. _____

11. Rob and Dick ran swiftly out the front door and through the gate. _____

12. They never returned to that empty old house. _____

B. Choose the correct adverb for each sentence.

finally	late	nervously	Suddenly

1. Dad's plane was arriving_____.

2. Mom kept glancing _____ at the clock in the airport.

3. _____ the gate lights flashed.

4. Dad's plane _____ had landed.

Adverbs That Compare

> ■ Add -er when using short adverbs to compare two actions.
>   EXAMPLE: Joe ran **faster** than Jill.
> ■ Add -est when using short adverbs to compare more than
>   two actions.
>   EXAMPLE: Jim ran **fastest** of all.
> ■ Use more or most with longer adverbs and with adverbs
>   that end in -ly when comparing two or more than two actions.
>   EXAMPLES: Rob answered **more quickly** than Sue. Tim
>   answered **most quickly** of all.

■ **Complete each sentence below by writing the correct form of the adverb shown in parentheses.**

1. (close)   Aunt Amy lives _____ to Lake Hope than we do.

2. (early)   She usually arrives there _____ than we do.

3. (fast)   Aunt Amy says that I can row _____ than anyone else on the lake.

4. (quickly)   But my cousin Jake can bait a hook _____ than I can.

5. (patiently)   And Aunt Amy can wait _____ than Jake and I put together.

6. (carefully)   Jake and I are both careful, but Aunt Amy baits the hook _____.

7. (quietly)   Jake and I try to see who can sit _____.

8. (soon)   I usually break the silence _____ than Jake.

9. (skillfully)   I'd have to admit that Aunt Amy fishes _____ of the three of us.

10. (happily)   And no one I know welcomes us to her home _____ than she does.

Adjectives or Adverbs

> - Remember that adjectives describe nouns or pronouns. Adjectives tell **what kind, which one,** or **how many.**
>   EXAMPLES: **blue** sky, **this** year, **several** pages
> - Remember that adverbs describe verbs. Adverbs tell **how, when, where,** or **how often.**
>   EXAMPLES: Walk **slowly.** Go **now.** Come **here.**

- **In the sentences below, underline each adjective. Circle each adverb.**

1. Three men were given licenses to hunt once on rugged Kodiak Island.
2. They had finally received permission to hunt the wild animals that live there.
3. Their purpose was different than the word <u>hunt</u> usually suggests.
4. The men were zoo hunters and would try to catch three bear cubs.
5. The young cubs would soon have a comfortable, new home at a distant zoo.
6. Once on the hilly island, the hopeful men quietly unpacked and then lay down for six hours of rest.
7. The next day, the men carefully scanned the rocky cliffs through powerful glasses.
8. They saw a huge brown bear with three cubs tumbling playfully around her.
9. The men spent two hours climbing quietly up to a point overlooking that ledge.
10. A large den could barely be seen in the rocks.
11. The wise men knew that bears never charge uphill.
12. However, the human scent immediately warned the watchful mother bear.
13. With a fierce roar, she walked heavily out of the cave and stared up at the men with her beady eyes.
14. One of the men tightly tied a red bandana and a dirty sock to a rope and threw the bundle down the slope.
15. The curious bear charged clumsily after it.
16. Quickly the men dropped to the wide ledge below.
17. But the wise cubs successfully hid from the men.

Prepositions

41

- A **preposition** is a word that shows the relationship of a noun or a pronoun to another word in the sentence.
    EXAMPLES: The cat **under** the tree is mine.
- Some prepositions include: <u>in</u>, <u>down</u>, <u>to</u>, <u>by</u>, <u>of</u>, <u>with</u>, <u>for</u>, and <u>at</u>.
- A **prepositional phrase** is a group of words that begins with a preposition and ends with a noun or a pronoun.
    EXAMPLES: **in** the house, **down** the street, **to** us

A. Underline the prepositional phrase in each sentence below. Circle the prepositions.

1. The box (on) the dining room table was wrapped.
2. A friend of Marta's was having a birthday.
3. Marta had been saving money for weeks so she could buy the present.
4. Now Marta was dressing in her bedroom.
5. Marta's little sister Tina toddled into the dining room.
6. She pulled the tablecloth, and the box fell to the floor.
7. Marta heard a thump and ran to the dining room.
8. Tina hid under the table.
9. The playful look on her face made Marta smile.

B. Underline ten prepositional phrases in the sentences below.

All fifth graders with perfect attendance will go to a baseball game in the spring. They will be driven to the ball park on the school bus. Tickets have been purchased for them by the principal. The parents of Sarah and Rick will go with the group. The children will be cheering loudly for the home team.

C. Give directions for a treasure hunt. Use the prepositional phrases below in your sentences.

around the corner	near the school	under a rock	beneath the tree

_____

_____

_____

_____

Unit 3, Grammar and Usage   **47**

> ▪ May expresses **permission.**
> EXAMPLE: **May** I go to town?
> ▪ Can expresses the **ability** to do something.
> EXAMPLE: She **can** play well.
> ▪ Good is an adjective. It tells **what kind.**
> EXAMPLE: My sister is a **good** cook.
> ▪ Well is an adverb. It tells **how.**
> EXAMPLE: Did you do **well** today?

▪ **Underline the correct word in each sentence below.**

1. (Can, May) I use the pen on your desk, Sam?

2. Yes, you (can, may) use it, but I doubt that you (can, may) make it work, Sara.

3. Look, Sam! It's working (good, well) now.

4. That's (good, well). How did you make it work?

5. (Can, May) we have an early appointment, Doctor Morris?

6. Just a moment. I'll see whether I (can, may) arrange that.

7. Yes, I believe that will work out (good, well).

8. Thank you, doctor. That will be (good, well) for my schedule, too.

9. Mr. Moore, (can, may) we have these stacks of old magazines?

10. Of course you (can, may), boys.

11. Are you sure you (can, may) carry them, though?

12. I (can, may) help you if they are too heavy for you.

13. Thank you, Mr. Moore, but I'm sure that we (can, may) manage very (good, well).

14. That's a (good, well) money-making project you have. What is the money being used for?

15. We're raising money for new school band uniforms, and we're doing quite (good, well), too.

16. Velma did a (good, well) job on her science project.

17. She did so (good, well) that she will take her project to the State Fair this summer.

18. She will also bring a guest with her, and she has a (good, well) idea who she will bring.

19. If Al (can, may), he will do a project and go with her.

> - <u>Teach</u> means "to give instruction to others."
>   EXAMPLE: Mrs. Gray will **teach** me to speak Spanish.
> - <u>Learn</u> means "to get knowledge."
>   EXAMPLE: I'm **learning** to speak Spanish.
> - <u>Set</u> means "to place something in a special position."
>   EXAMPLE: Please **set** the books on the table.
> - <u>Sit</u> means "to take a resting position."
>   EXAMPLE: Please **sit** down and rest for a minute.

- **Underline the correct word in each sentence below.**

1. Andy: Who will (learn, teach) you to play the piano?

2. Pat: I hope to (learn, teach) from my older sister, Beth.

3. Andy: Wouldn't it be better to have Mrs. Hill (learn, teach) you?

4. Pat: You were quite small when she began to (learn, teach) you.

5. Pat: Was it hard to (learn, teach) when you were so young?

6. Andy: Yes, but Mrs. Hill let me (set, sit) on a high, round stool.

7. Andy: At home I would (set, sit) a thick book on the piano bench and (set, sit) on it.

8. Andy: Then I grew enough so that I could (set, sit) on the bench and still reach the keys.

9. Liz: Beth asked Dad to (learn, teach) her how to drive.

10. Liz: She says it would make her nervous to have someone that she didn't know (learn, teach) her.

11. Tom: Are you going to go along and (set, sit) in the back seat?

12. Liz: I doubt that Beth will want me to (set, sit) anywhere near when she is driving.

13. Isaac: Martha, I am going to (learn, teach) you a new skill.

14. Isaac: I know you are old enough to (learn, teach) how to (set, sit) the table.

15. Isaac: (Set, Sit) there, Martha, so that you can watch me.

16. Isaac: First I (set, sit) the plates in their places.

17. Isaac: Then I put a glass at each place where someone will (set, sit).

18. Isaac: Once I (learn, teach) you everything, you will be able to (set, sit) the table every night.

19. Martha: Good! Let me try to (set, sit) it now.

A. Write each noun, pronoun, verb, and adjective from the sentences below in the proper column.

1. Kathy had found Ray's black notebook.
2. She gave it to him on Thursday.
3. He was thankful.

NOUNS	PRONOUNS	VERBS	ADJECTIVES
_____	_____	_____	_____
_____	_____	_____	_____
_____	_____	_____	_____
_____	_____	_____	_____

B. Underline each verb or verb phrase in the present tense. Circle each verb or verb phrase in the past tense. Then write the future tense of each verb.

1. On that television series, we study people of other lands.   _____

2. On the first program we learned about the people of Egypt.   _____

3. Old records tell us that the people plowed with a crooked stick.   _____
_____

4. They grew crops in the sand.   _____

5. Some farmers raised wheat and barley.   _____

C. Underline each prepositional phrase. Circle each adverb.

1. These special horses still display their skill in Austria.
2. These noble, white stallions are perfectly trained by experts.
3. They perform beautifully with their riders in the Riding Hall.
4. The eight horses and riders gracefully present a "horse ballet" in perfect time.
5. The great stallion Pluto stands on his back legs and leaps upward.

A. Underline the correct word in each sentence below.

1. A blind person (doesn't, don't) have to depend on another person.
2. Dog trainers (can, may) teach dogs to be their dependable guides.
3. These dogs leave (their, theirs) kennels at ten weeks of age.
4. Each puppy stays in a 4-H club (members, member's) home.
5. One member, Karen, had (her, hers) puppy, Koko, for twelve months.
6. Karen had always (wanted, will want) a puppy to take care of.
7. But, Karen had to realize that Koko was not really (her, hers).
8. "Koko and (I, me) hated to say goodbye," Karen said.
9. "It was hard to tell which one of us was (sadder, saddest)."
10. Karen had (learned, taught) Koko to walk on a leash and to display normal, (good, well) behavior.
11. The kennel owner said Karen had done her job (good, well).
12. He knew that Koko could now (learn, teach) to guide a blind person.
13. Now Karen (goes, went) to the kennel every week to visit Koko.
14. She has (took, taken) a treat for him each time, and Koko always wags his tail to say thank-you.
15. Koko is (largest, larger) each time Karen sees him.

B. Read the paragraph below. Find and underline the eight errors in grammar and usage. In the space above the sentences, write the correction.

The state of Kentucky is called the Bluegrass State because of

its bluish-colored grass. Rivers form a large part of Kentuckys

borders. The Ohio River is one of the longer rivers of any

in the United States. Kentucky also have many natural lakes.

Spring is the rainier season, and fall is the driest season.

Louisville are Kentucky's larger city. Louisville is the home

of the famous horse race, the Kentucky Derby.

Louisville has the name of King Louis XVI of France.

Him helped during the American Revolution. All around,

Kentucky is one of the prettier of our fifty states.

C. In the paragraph below, underline each adjective. Circle each adverb.

The circus is an exciting show to see. It has been called
"The Greatest Show on Earth." Smiling children walk happily
with Mom or Dad into the huge tent. They find seats
quickly because the brass band is starting to play. The
colorful parade will begin in three minutes. First comes the
ringmaster in his bright red coat and tall hat, parading
importantly to the center ring.

D. Complete this paragraph about the circus by writing adjectives or adverbs in the blanks.

Next the _____ band plays _____. The

_____ bareback riders follow. Their horses walk _____.

They help their riders keep their balance. Next are the _____

elephants. Each walks _____ with a _____ young rider sitting

on its _____ head. The tigers snarl _____ as they pace

around in their _____ cages. Everyone wants to see the _____

clowns do their _____ tricks.

E. Write the correct possessive form of each noun in parentheses.

1. (school)   The _____ spring play has been planned.

2. (students)   All of the _____ parts have been chosen.

3. (childrens)   Some of the _____ mothers will make costumes.

4. (director)   The _____ job will go to Miss Andrews.

5. (Villagers)   The title of the play is "The _____ Mystery."

F. Underline the correct word in parentheses in each sentence below.

1. The mystery of the play is the (harder, hardest) to solve
   of any mystery I've read.

2. Why does the sun shine (brighter, brightest) in that village
   than at the other village?

3. This play has a (more, most) surprising ending than the other play.

> - **Capitalize** the first word of a sentence.
>   EXAMPLE: Many students have pen pals.
> - Capitalize the first word of a direct quotation.
>   EXAMPLE: Jane asked, "Where does your pen pal live?"

A. Circle each letter that should be capitalized. Write the capital letter above it.

1. "have you met your pen pal?" I asked.

2. john answered, "yes, he spent the holidays with me."

3. so I've invited my pen pal to visit me.

4. he hopes to arrive in the United States next June.

5. i am making many plans for his visit.

6. we're going to hike in the mountains.

> - Capitalize the first word of every line of poetry.
>   EXAMPLE: There was a monkey climbed up a tree;
>   When he fell down, then down fell he.
> - Capitalize the first, last, and all important words in the titles of books, poems, stories, and songs.
>   EXAMPLE: Who wrote *Little House on the Prairie?*

B. Circle each letter that should be capitalized. Write the capital letter above it.

1. there was an old woman

   lived under a hill,

   and if she's not gone,

   she lives there still.

2. if all the world were water,

   and all the water were ink,

   what should we do for bread and cheese?

   and what should we do for drink?

3. Have you read Longfellow's poem "the song of hiawatha"?

4. Our class is learning the song "down by the river."

5. If you're interested in ballooning, read *up, up and away.*

6. Mike wrote a story called "a birthday balloon ride."

Capitalizing Proper Nouns and Adjectives

- Capitalize all proper nouns.
  EXAMPLES: Main Street, Germany, Atlantic Ocean, Friday, Florida, Rocky Mountains, Halloween, December, Aunt Ann, Mom, Holmes School, James
- A proper adjective is an adjective that is made from a proper noun. Capitalize all proper adjectives.
  EXAMPLES: the English language, Italian dishes, French people, American tourists, the Australian cities

A. Circle each letter that should be capitalized. Write the capital letter above it.

1. My uncle larry had just returned from a world trip.

2. He brought gifts for everyone in our family, including our
   dog, chipper.

3. He gave mom some delicate japanese dishes that he
   bought in tokyo, japan.

4. He gave my sister a scottish plaid kilt like the bagpipers
   wear in scotland.

5. dad really likes the hat uncle larry got for him in london.

6. The hat reminds us of the kind sherlock holmes wore.

7. My gift was an african drum from mali in west africa.

8. uncle larry told us how delicious the italian food was.

9. chipper's gift was a colorful, embroidered dog jacket
   from thailand.

**B. Write four sentences about a trip you would like to take.
Use proper nouns and at least one proper adjective in the sentences.**

1. _____
2. _____
3. _____
4. _____

Capitalizing Titles and Abbreviations

- Capitalize a person's title when it comes before a name.
  EXAMPLES: Mayor Thomas, Governor Swanson
- Capitalize abbreviations of titles.
  EXAMPLES: Dr. Norris; Mr. and Mrs. J. B. Benton, Jr.;
  Ms. Harris; Mr. John F. Lynch, Sr.

A. Circle each letter that should be capitalized. Write the capital letter above it.

1. We saw governor potter and senator williams in their

   offices.

2. They were discussing a state health problem with dr. laura

   bedford and commissioner phillips.

3. We ate lunch with rev. barton and mr. james adams, jr.

4. They are part of a committee planning a welcome for prince

   charles of England, who will tour our state next month.

- Capitalize abbreviations of days and months, parts of addresses, and titles of members of the armed forces. Also capitalize all letters in abbreviations for states.
  EXAMPLES: Mon.; Sept.; 501 N. Elm St.; Capt. W. R. Russell; Chicago, IL

B. Circle each letter that should be capitalized. Write the capital letter above it.

1. gen. david e. morgan

   6656 n. second ave.

   evanston, il 60202

2. valentine's day Exhibit

   at oak grove library

   mon.—fri., feb 10—14

   101 e. madison st.

3. sgt. carlos m. martinez

   1602 water st.

   minneapolis, mn 55350

4. maxwell school Field Day

   wed., apr. 30, 1:00

   Register mon.—tues., apr. 28—29

   mr. modica's office

> ■ Use a **period** at the end of a declarative sentence.
>   EXAMPLE: The lens is an important part of a camera.
> ■ Use a **question mark** at the end of an interrogative sentence.
>   EXAMPLE: Do you enjoy having your picture taken?

A. Add the correct end punctuation to each sentence below.

1. Picture-taking is an exciting hobby for many people

2. My dad is one of those people

3. Have you ever gone on a vacation with a camera bug

4. Mom and I love Dad's photos

5. But getting those really good shots can be tiring

6. Can you imagine waiting in the hot desert sun while Dad
   gets just the right angle on a cactus

7. Or have you ever sat in the car while your dad waited
   for a grazing elk to turn its head

8. I don't need so much time when I take pictures

9. Of course my pictures aren't always as good as Dad's

B. Add the correct end punctuation where needed in the paragraphs below.

Have you ever wondered what it would be like to live as
our country's pioneers did___ You can visit log homes made to
look like the original cabins of pioneer days___ Then you can
see how difficult life was for the pioneers who helped our
country grow___

The cabins were small and roughly built___ Many cabins had
just one room___ Where was the kitchen___ Most of the cooking was
done in the large fireplace___ The fireplace also supplied the
only heat___ Wasn't it cold___ You can be sure the winter winds
whistled between the logs___ And where did the pioneers sleep___
Most cabins had a ladder reaching up to the bedroom loft___

The furniture in the cabins was usually as roughly built as
the cabins themselves___ All the clothing was handmade by the
family___ They ate food grown and caught on their land___ Would
you have liked to live in those times___

> ■ Use a period at the end of an imperative sentence.
>   EXAMPLE: Please sign your name here.
> ■ Use an **exclamation point** at the end of an exclamatory sentence.
>   EXAMPLE: What a wonderful time we had at the show!

C. Add the correct end punctuation to each sentence below.

1. The children were admiring their new kites___
2. Jack thought, "What a great day for kite-flying it is___".
3. He said, "Please get some string___"
4. Susan asked, "Don't you think it's a little too windy___"
5. Jack answered, "What a silly question that is___"
6. "How can it be too windy to fly a kite___"
7. "Wind is just what we need___"
8. Susan insisted, "Have you forgotten the time that your kite was torn to shreds by the wind___"
9. Jack answered, "That was just a junky little kite I made myself___"
10. "Let's go then," said Susan. "What fun it will be___"
11. A short time later we heard the cry, "Oh, no___"
12. Can you guess whose kite was carried away by the wind and caught in a tree___

D. Add the correct end punctuation where needed in the paragraphs below.

Have you ever seen pictures of northern Minnesota___ It is a region of many lakes___ My family once spent a week on Little Birch Lake___ What a sight it was___

There were thousands of white birches reflected in the blue water___ The fishing was great___ Every day we caught large numbers of bass, and every night we cooked fresh fish for our dinner___

The nearest town was Hackensack___ At the waterfront was a large statue of Diana Marie Kensack___ She is seated at the water's edge___ Her gaze is fixed on the horizon___ Do you know who she was___ Legends say that she was Paul Bunyan's sweetheart___ She is still waiting at the shore for him to come back to her___ Be sure to visit Diana when you are in Minnesota___

> - Use **quotation marks** to show the exact words of a speaker. Use a comma or other punctuation marks to separate the quotation from the rest of the sentence.
>   EXAMPLE: "Who made this delicious candy?" asked Claire.
> - A quotation may be placed at the beginning or the end of a sentence. It may also be divided within the sentence.
>   EXAMPLES: Lawrence said, "Let's play checkers."
>   "My brother," said Mildred, "brought me this ring."

A. Add quotation marks to each sentence below.

1. We will read about a great inventor today, said Miss Davis.

2. Let me see, Miss Davis went on, whether you can guess who the inventor is.

3. Will you give us some clues? asked Chris.

4. Yes, answered Miss Davis, and here is the first clue.

5. His inventions have made our lives easier and more pleasant, said Miss Davis.

6. Is it Alexander Graham Bell? asked Judy.

7. Mr. Bell did give us the telephone, said Miss Davis, but he is not the man I have in mind.

8. This man gave us another kind of machine that talks, Miss Davis said.

9. It must be Thomas Alva Edison and the phonograph, said Jerry.

10. You are right, Miss Davis said.

B. Place quotation marks and other punctuation where needed in the sentences below.

1. Polly asked Where will you spend the holidays, Aunt Mae?

2. We plan to drive to Uncle Henry's ranch said Aunt Mae.

3. Polly asked Won't it be quite cold?

4. Yes said Aunt Mae but it will be so much fun to slide down the hill behind the house.

5. And it's great fun to go into the woods and cut down a Christmas tree added Cousin Bob.

6. Come with us said Aunt Mae.

- Use an **apostrophe** in a contraction to show where a letter or letters have been taken out.
  EXAMPLE: I **can't** be there until three o'clock.
- Use an apostrophe to form a possessive noun. Add -'s to most singular nouns. Add -' to most plural nouns.
  EXAMPLE: Mike's gym shoes are high tops. The boys' gym suits are blue and white.

- **Write the word or words in which an apostrophe has been left out. Insert the apostrophe.**

1. Do you remember Aesops fables?   _____Aesop's_____

2. The stories lessons came at the end.   _____

3. Mrs. Clarks class was talking about these stories.   _____

4. Wendy liked the story about the fox and the crow,   _____

   but she couldnt remember the storys lesson.   _____

5. "Thats the one that says you shouldnt be too proud   _____

   after people praise you," said Dick.   _____

6. Wong's favorite wasnt as well-known.   _____

7. It told about a tiny gnats great pride.   _____

8. While sitting on a bulls horn the gnat said, "Please   _____

   tell me if Im too heavy."   _____

9. "I can't even tell youre there," replied the bull.   _____

10. The lesson is that sometimes a persons view of   _____

    himself or herself isnt a true one.   _____

11. Dwaynes story told about a donkey that dressed   _____

    itself in a lions skin.   _____

12. But the donkey still couldnt scare the fox.   _____

13. Dwayne said the lesson is that a persons fine   _____

    clothes dont make the person any better.   _____

> ■ Use a **comma** between words or word groups in a series.
>   EXAMPLE: Food, medical supplies, blankets, and clothing were rushed to the flooded area.
> ■ Use a comma to separate the parts of a compound sentence.
>   EXAMPLE: Many homes were flooded, and the owners were taken to safety in boats.

A. Add commas where needed in the sentences below.

1. The heavy rain caused flooding in Cedarville Taylorville Gardner and other towns along the Cedar River.
2. The flood washed away bridges roads and some small homes.
3. Our home had water in the basement and most of our neighbors' homes did, too.
4. We spent the night bailing mopping and worrying.
5. We put our washer and dryer up on blocks and then we helped Mrs. Wilson.
6. Some of our shrubs flowers and small trees may have to be replaced.
7. Mrs. Wilson's newly-planted vegetable garden was washed away and the Smiths lost their shed.
8. The people in our neighborhood were very lucky and everyone agreed that the flood brought us closer together.

> ■ Use a comma to separate a direct quotation from the rest of a sentence.
>   EXAMPLE: "We're leaving now," said Ann. Ann said, "It's time to go."

B. Add commas where needed in the sentences below.

1. Sally asked "Why did the rooster cross the road?"
2. "To get to the other side " answered Terry.
3. "That's really an old joke " Terry added.
4. Sally asked "Do you know a newer one?"
5. Terry asked "What holds the moon up?"
6. "Moon beams " said Terry.

> ■ Use a comma to set off the name of a person who is addressed.
>   EXAMPLE: "Alan, can't you go with us?" asked Bill.
> ■ Use a comma to set off words like yes, no, well, and oh when they begin a sentence.
>   EXAMPLE: "No, I have to visit my aunt," answered Alan.

C. Add commas where needed in the sentences below.

1. "Melody and Tim would you like to go to the hockey game?" Aunt Marie asked.
2. "Oh yes!" Tim exclaimed.
3. "Aunt Marie I'd love to," called Melody.
4. "Well it's settled children," said Aunt Marie.
5. "Ted did you go to the model show last night?" asked Sam.
6. "No I couldn't make it," answered Ted.
7. "Oh I was going to ask if Carlos won a prize," Sam said.
8. "Well I hope so," Ted said.
9. "Well then," Sam said, "let's call and ask him."
10. "Carlos did you win a prize last night?" Sam asked.
11. "Yes I did," replied Carlos.
12. "Oh what did you win?" asked Sam.
13. "Well you'd never guess," answered Carlos.
14. "Carlos don't keep us guessing," said Sam.
15. "Well you know my model was of a helicopter. My prize was a ride in a helicopter!" exclaimed Carlos.

D. Pretend that you and your friends are planning an outing. Write a conversation that might take place between you and your friends. Use the names of the persons being addressed. In some sentences, use yes, no, oh, or well. Punctuate your sentences correctly.

_____

_____

_____

_____

_____

_____

A. Circle each letter that should be capitalized. Write the capital letter above it.

1. last summer we toured montana and wyoming.

2. my brother bob liked hiking in the grand teton mountains.

3. the trip down the snake river was my favorite part.

4. we spotted two american bald eagles.

5. my mom liked glacier park and the rocky mountains best.

6. dad bought a book named *tales of the old west.*

7. dr. vicenik is governor adams's personal doctor.

8. mrs. vicenik and mr. morrison are brother and sister.

9. ms. louis has invited dr. vicenik's son to speak to our class.

10. our class made a poster with this information on it:

    walter vicenik will speak

    at winston school

    on tues., apr. 25 at 3:00

B. Add commas and quotation marks where needed in the sentences below.

1. Do you skate? George asked.
2. Yes! several voices exclaimed.
3. George said Everyone who skates or wants to learn how is invited to a party.
4. Peggy asked What do we have to bring?
5. Bring bus fare some money for snacks and money for skate rental George answered.
6. We'll skate for a couple of hours and then we'll go to my house for pizza George explained.
7. I'll bet it's your birthday Susan said.
8. It's next week but I wasn't planning to tell anyone George said.

Using What You've Learned

A. Correct the story below. Circle each letter that should be capitalized. Add missing periods, question marks, exclamation points, commas, quotation marks, or apostrophes where needed. Be sure to write the correct end punctuation on the blank after each sentence.

have you ever read eugene fields poem, "the duel"___
The chinese plate and the old dutch clock told the story
to a poet___ they were hanging above the fireplace and
they could see the gingham dog and the calico cat sitting
on the table___

the gingham dog said bow-wow-wow___

mee-ow answered the calico cat___

then the dog and the cat began to fight___ bits of gingham
and calico were scattered everywhere___

the chinese plate cried oh what can we do___
but the dog and cat continued to tumble and fight all night___
the next morning there was no trace of dog or cat___

many people said burglars must have stolen them___
but the old chinese plate said to the poet they ate each
other up and thats the truth___

what a surprise ending that was___

B. Make corrections in the story below as you did in Exercise A.

There is a russian folk tale named "the coming of the snow
maid___" it tells about winter in russia where winter is very
long and very cold___

ivan, a peasant, and his wife, marie, had no children___ they
often watched their neighbors children at play in the snow___
one day marie got an idea___

ivan lets make a snow child she said___ we can pretend
it is our own___

the snow child came alive and they called her Snow Maid___
she grew rapidly until early june___ then she disappeared
in a tiny cloud___

dont cry marie said ivan___ Snow Maid has returned to the
sky but she will come back to us next september___

C. Correct the story below. Circle each letter that should be capitalized. Write the capital letter above it. Add missing periods, commas, quotation marks, or apostrophes where needed. Be sure to write the correct end punctuation on the blank after each sentence.

A World War II hero, general dwight david eisenhower, became

president eisenhower___ in his youth, he was just one of

six eisenhower boys___ he and his brothers arthur edgar earl

roy and milton grew up on the edge of abilene, kansas___

All the boys had chores to do, morning noon and night___ One

of the older brothers chores was to push the youngest brothers

baby buggy___ dwight, or ike, as he was called, would

lie on the floor while reading a book, and push and

pull the buggy back and forth with his feet___

his mother once said ike was good at hoeing___ he hoed the

garden of beans peas potatoes corn cabbage carrots and

beets___ the boys went to lincoln school she said and always played

baseball in the schoolyard___ she often had to patch ikes pants

as a result of his sliding into home plate___

all the brothers liked to read___ ike enjoyed greek and

roman history and stories about military leaders___ his

high school classmates thought he would become a history

teacher at yale university___

D. Write a paragraph about one of our national heroes or someone you know and admire. Follow all the rules of capitalization and punctuation.

_____

_____

_____

_____

Writing Sentences

- Every sentence has a base. The **sentence base** is made up of a simple subject and a simple predicate.
  EXAMPLE: Girls stared.
- Add other words to the sentence base to expand the meaning of the sentence.
  EXAMPLE: The **bewildered** girls stared **in amazement at the mysterious light.**

A. Expand the meaning of each sentence base below. Add adjectives, adverbs, and/or prepositional phrases. Write your expanded sentence.

1. (Plane flew.) _____

2. (Creatures ran.) _____

3. (Dogs played.) _____

4. (Police chased.) _____

5. (Boys discovered.) _____

B. Imagine two different scenes for each sentence base below. Write an expanded sentence to describe each scene you imagine.

1. (Children explored.)   a. _____

   b. _____

2. (Fire was set.)   a. _____

   b. _____

3. (Crowd roared.)   a. _____

   b. _____

4. (Wind blew.)   a. _____

   b. _____

5. (Friend sent.)   a. _____

   b. _____

6. (Clown was dressed.)   a. _____

   b. _____

> ■ A **topic sentence** is a sentence that states the main idea of
> a paragraph. EXAMPLE: **Many of the best things in life
> are free.** The sun and the moon give their light without
> charge. A true friend can't be bought. The beauty of the
> clouds in a blue sky is there for all to enjoy.

A. Write a topic sentence for each of the paragraphs below.

1. During the baseball season, Rob played every day after
   school. He attended as many ball games as possible to see
   how the pros played. He read many books and magazines about
   the game. He was determined to try out for the big leagues
   as soon as he was old enough.

   TOPIC SENTENCE: _____

2. During the day, we have fun. Our whole family gets
   together. We watch the parade in the morning. Then we go
   swimming or have a picnic. And we always have watermelon
   to eat. But most of all, we enjoy watching the fireworks
   display in the park at night.

   TOPIC SENTENCE: _____

3. There are many parks to enjoy. Museums and aquariums
   have interesting exhibits. Large stores and malls have
   a great selection of things to buy. Many large cities also
   have major sports teams to watch.

   TOPIC SENTENCE: _____

**B. Choose one of the topics below. Write a topic sentence for it. Then
write a paragraph of about fifty words in which you develop the topic.**

The most useful invention   My favorite holiday (other than the Fourth of July)

A frightening experience   A place I want to visit

_____

_____

_____

_____

_____

_____

Writing Supporting Details

> ■ Sentences that contain **supporting details** develop the topic sentence of a paragraph. The details may be facts, examples, or reasons.

A. Read the topic sentence below. Then read the numbered sentences. Underline the four sentences that contain details that support the topic sentence.

TOPIC SENTENCE: Our school is planning a Fun Fair.

1. Each class will be responsible for one part of the Fun Fair.
2. Some schools sell magazines to raise money.
3. Our class will make and sell popcorn.
4. Parents and teachers will help.
5. Popcorn is a healthful snack.
6. The money raised will be used to buy audiovisual equipment.

B. Underline the correct word to complete the sentence.

The supporting details in the sentences above were (facts, examples, reasons).

C. Choose one of the topic sentences. Write it on the first line. Then write three sentences that contain supporting details. The details may be facts, examples, or reasons.

1. Having a pet is a lot of work.
2. A large (or small) family has advantages.
3. My vacation (in the mountains, at camp, on the seashore, or other place) was fun.
4. Every student should have an allowance.

_____

_____

_____

_____

D. Fill in the blank below with the word facts, examples, or reasons.

The supporting details in my paragraph were _____.

> ■ **Comparing** two objects, persons, or ideas shows the likenesses between them. Comparing expresses a thought in a colorful, interesting way.
>   EXAMPLE: Walking lets the walker be as free as a bird that has flown from its cage.
> ■ **Contrasting** two objects, persons, or ideas shows the differences between them. Contrasting can also express a thought in a colorful, interesting way.
>   EXAMPLE: Baby Rachel's morning mood is one of sunshine, rainbows, and laughter. Her nap-time mood, however, suggests gathering clouds.

A. Read each topic sentence and the pair of sentences that follow. Underline the sentence that expresses a supporting detail in a colorful, interesting way.

1. TOPIC SENTENCE: Having the flu is no fun.

   a. Pat was tired of being in bed with the flu.

   b. After a week in bed with the flu, Pat felt like her pet hamster, Hamby, spinning his wheel in his cage.

2. TOPIC SENTENCE: Koalas aren't all they seem to be.

   a. A koala is cute but unfriendly.

   b. A koala looks like a cuddly teddy bear, but it is about as friendly as a grizzly bear.

B. Rewrite each sentence below in a more colorful, interesting way. Use comparison or contrast.

1. A mosquito bite is itchy.

   _____

2. Taking a bus to school is fun.

   _____

3. Dogs are friendlier than cats.

   _____

4. Reading is a good way to spend your free time.

   _____

5. Stealing a base makes baseball exciting.

   _____

> ■ Supporting details can be arranged in order of location.
> EXAMPLE: The sofa was **on the long wall to your right.**
> A table sat **at either end** of the sofa.

A. In the paragraph below, underline the words that show location.

I stood watching. <u>Below me</u> was the playground. Across the street from the playground, men were building an apartment house. Cement trucks were lined up along the street. They were delivering concrete for the basement walls of the apartment house. A kindergarten class was playing dodge ball inside the playground. The wise teacher told the class to move closer to the school.

B. Choose one of the scenes or objects below. Write a topic sentence about it. Then write a paragraph of at least five sentences describing the scene or object. Use words such as <u>above</u>, <u>ahead</u>, <u>around</u>, <u>behind</u>, <u>next to</u>, <u>on top of</u>, and <u>under</u> to show location.

Scenes: your classroom, your room at home, a garden
Objects: your bicycle, a car, the American flag

_____

_____

_____

_____

_____

_____

_____

_____

_____

_____

C. Underline the words you used to show location.

> - The **topic** of a paragraph should be something the writer is interested in or familiar with.
>   EXAMPLES: school, animals, science, sports, hobbies
> - The **title** should be based on the topic.
> - The **audience** is the person or people who will read what is written.
>   EXAMPLES: classmates, readers of the class newspaper, family members

A. Suppose that the topic chosen is <u>sports</u>. Underline the sports topic below which you would most like to write about.

1. Is winning the most important thing in sports?

2. There are many reasons why tennis (or baseball, or swimming, or _____) is my favorite sport.

3. Sports can be an enjoyable family activity.

B. Think about the topic you underlined in Exercise A. Underline the audience below that you would like to write for.

1. your parents

2. a coach

3. your best friend

C. Write a paragraph of about seventy words, using the sentence you underlined in Exercise A as your topic sentence. Write a title for your paragraph. Direct your paragraph to the audience you underlined in Exercise B.

_____

_____

_____

_____

_____

_____

_____

■ **Clustering** uses a special drawing that shows how ideas relate to one main topic. That topic is written in a center shape. Other shapes contain the ideas. Lines show how the ideas are connected to the main topic.

EXAMPLE:

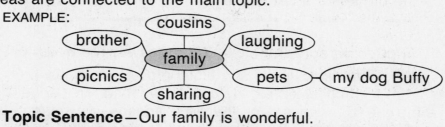

Topic Sentence—Our family is wonderful.

A. Complete each cluster below by writing words that the topic makes you think of. You may add additional shapes and connecting lines.

1.

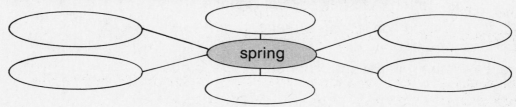

TOPIC SENTENCE: _____

2.

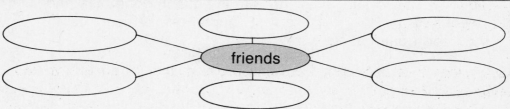

TOPIC SENTENCE: _____

B. Choose one of the topics in Exercise A. Write it on the title line below. Then write your topic sentence for that topic. Complete the paragraph.

_____

_____

_____

_____

_____

_____

A Descriptive Paragraph

■ A **descriptive paragraph** describes something. It is made colorful and interesting through the use of details.
  EXAMPLE: A **thick coating** of dust covered everything in the **old abandoned** house.

A. Read the descriptive paragraph below. Then answer the question.

In my neighborhood, there is a small grocery store just a block from my house. An elderly couple, Mr. and Mrs. Aggens, are the owners. I always hope that Mrs. Aggens will wait on me. She is friendly and full of smiles. She always gives me extra large scoops of ice cream. She doesn't hurry me when I can't decide whether to spend my money on apples or fruit bars. After I make my purchase, I like to stay, smell the freshly ground coffee, and talk to Mrs. Aggens.

1. What kind of person is Mrs. Aggens? Underline the words that describe her.

crabby, patient, impatient, kind, stingy, generous

B. Read the paragraph below about the same store.

In my neighborhood, there is a store near our house. The owners are a husband and wife. The wife is patient, generous, and friendly. Near the door is a fruit counter and an ice cream counter. I often shop there.

1. List at least five details that are missing from this paragraph. _____

_____

_____

2. What is the result of leaving out these details? _____

_____

C. Write a descriptive paragraph about a place you visit often. Use details to make your paragraph colorful and interesting.

_____

_____

_____

_____

_____

Writing a Descriptive Paragraph

> - Writers use **descriptive words** that tell how something looks, feels, smells, tastes, or sounds.
>   EXAMPLE: The **shady** forest was dressed in the **soft greens** and **pale yellows** of early spring.
> - Writers use verbs that tell exactly what someone is doing or how someone moves.
>   EXAMPLE: Richard **tramped** across the newly mopped kitchen floor.

A. Read the paragraph below and answer the questions that follow.

> Jody stood silently at the rickety gate of Uncle Harry's weathered old ranch house. The crooked gate hung on only its top hinge. The house that had never known a paint brush seemed to have whitened with age. A gentle breeze rippled the tall grass and filled Jody's nostrils with the sugary smell of sweet peas. Jody turned. Yes, there were those lovely white, pastel pink, and lavender blooms. But everything else had faded with age.

1. What words tell how the ranch house looked? _____

   how the gate looked? _____

2. What word tells how the breeze felt? _____

   how the grass looked? _____ how it moved? _____

   how the sweet peas smelled? _____ how they looked? _____

B. Choose a familiar place to write about in a descriptive paragraph. Write a topic sentence to begin the paragraph. Think about how the place looks, the sounds you might hear there, the smells you might smell there, how it feels to be there, and the things you might taste there. Write descriptive sentences that tell about these things to complete your paragraph.

_____

_____

_____

_____

_____

A. Expand the meaning of each sentence base below. Add adjectives, adverbs, and/or prepositional phrases. Write your expanded sentence.

1. (Lifeguard swam.) _____

2. (Kitten climbed.) _____

3. (Team celebrated.) _____

B. Write a topic sentence for the paragraph below.

> My brothers and I put on our warmest clothes and went outside. We started building walls of snow blocks. We piled up lots of snowballs. Then we threw the snowballs at the telephone pole in the alley. After a long day in Fort Snow, we went indoors and drank hot chocolate.

TOPIC SENTENCE: _____

C. Read the topic sentence below. Then underline the three sentences that contain details supporting the idea of the topic sentence.

TOPIC SENTENCE: Automobile seat belts save lives.

1. The first seat belts did not have shoulder straps.
2. A seat belt helps keep a front-seat passenger from going through the windshield.
3. A passenger who doesn't fasten his or her seat belt may be hurt if the car is in an accident.
4. Seat belts protect small children from falls and bumps while riding in the back seat.

D. For each sentence below, write a sentence that states the thought in a more colorful, interesting way. Use comparison or contrast.

1. The sky is pretty at sunset. _____

_____

2. My room needs cleaning. _____

_____

A. Complete the cluster below. Write a title for the topic. Then write a topic sentence and three sentences that contain supporting details.

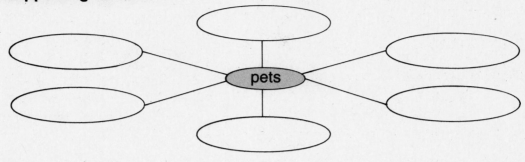

_____

TOPIC SENTENCE: _____

_____

_____

_____

B. Write a paragraph of at least four sentences describing your school gymnasium, art room, or science room. Use location words such as <u>above</u>, <u>ahead</u>, <u>around</u>, <u>behind</u>, <u>next to</u>, <u>on top of</u>, and <u>under</u>.

_____

_____

_____

_____

C. Fill in the blanks in the paragraph below with descriptive words and action verbs that make the paragraph colorful and interesting.

The _____ colt pulled itself up on its _____

legs. Then it _____ after its mother. Just as the colt

neared the fence, a _____, _____ rabbit

_____ under the fence and _____ up to the colt.

The startled colt _____ and let out a _____ neigh.

Its _____ mother _____ up to its side _____.

D. Choose one of the topic sentences below. Write a paragraph of four sentences, using <u>reasons</u> to support the thought of the topic sentence.

    1. Everyone should learn to swim.
    2. Report cards are necessary.
    3. Summer vacations are just the right length of time.

_____

_____

_____

_____

E. Choose one of the topic sentences below. Write a paragraph of four sentences, using <u>examples</u> to support the thought of the topic sentence.

    1. Many television programs are educational.
    2. Electrical inventions have made our lives easier.
    3. A hobby is more than a way to take up time.

_____

_____

_____

_____

F. Suppose that you have been given the general topic <u>hobbies</u> to write about. Before beginning to write, follow the steps below.

    1. Choose a hobby with which you are familiar or in which you are interested. Write a title for your paragraph.

_____

    2. Write the audience to whom you will address your paragraph.

_____

    3. Write a topic sentence. _____

    4. Write three sentences that support the thought of your topic sentence.

_____

_____

_____

> ■ When following written **directions,** it is important to read each step carefully. Be sure you have completed one step before going on to the next step.

■ **Read the recipe below. Then answer the questions that follow it.**

Peanut Butter Balls

½ cup wheat germ   ½ cup powdered milk
½ cup sunflower seeds   ½ cup honey
½ cup peanut butter   ½ cup sesame seeds (if desired)

a. Spread wheat germ and sunflower seeds on a cookie sheet. Bake at 350° for 15 minutes, stirring every 5 minutes.

b. Place toasted wheat germ and sunflower seeds in a bowl.

c. Add all other ingredients except sesame seeds. Mix well.

d. Form into balls, using 1 teaspoonful of dough for each ball.

e. Roll balls in sesame seeds. (This step is not necessary.)

f. Chill for 3 hours.

g. Serve as a tasty, good-for-you snack or dessert.

1. What is the recipe for? _____

2. What kitchen utensils are needed? _____

3. What quantity of each ingredient is needed? _____

4. What ingredients are used in step a? _____

5. What should the oven temperature be? _____

6. How long should the wheat germ and sunflower seeds

   be baked? _____

7. How often should you stir the wheat germ and sunflower seeds

   while they are baking? _____

8. How much dough is needed to form each ball? _____

9. How long should the peanut butter balls be chilled before

   eating? _____

10. Which ingredient may be left out? _____

> ■ **Alphabetical order** is used in many kinds of listings.
>   EXAMPLE: Miss Clark's class list: Adams, Coss, Edwards,
>   Gutierrez, Lee, Ortega, Shapiro, Turner

A. Complete each sentence below.

1. The letter n comes after _____ and before _____.

2. The letters between s and w are _____.

3. After e, the next four letters are _____.

4. The letters between i and m are _____.

5. The letters between e and j are _____.

6. The letter y comes after _____ and before _____.

7. The letters between l and r are _____.

8. After h, the next three letters are _____.

9. The letter g comes after _____ and before _____.

10. The letter t comes after _____ and before _____.

11. The last four letters of the alphabet are _____.

12. After v, the next two letters are _____.

13. The letters between n and s are _____.

14. The letters between m and r are _____.

15. After q, the next four letters are _____.

16. The letters between o and t are _____.

17. The first three letters after u are _____.

18. The letter before f is _____.

B. Write the first names of some of your classmates in alphabetical order.

_____   _____

_____   _____

_____   _____

> ■ Entries in a dictionary or an encyclopedia appear in alphabetical order, according to their first letters, second letters, third letters, and so on.
>   EXAMPLE: wave, wax, web, weed, wish, wisp

C. Number the words in each group in alphabetical order.

    3   4   2   1
1. whale, where, weary, water

2. school, second, safety, sailor

3. earth, ease, each, earn

4. recess, rain, ring, rose

5. elbow, eight, enamel, editor

6. cardinal, carrot, color, candy

7. gentle, gather, globe, gallon

8. mason, master, mascot, mash

9. leaf, learn, listen, loan

10. vegetable, varnish, violin, valentine

D. Number the entries in each column in the order of their appearance in an encyclopedia.

1. _____ Bell, Alexander Graham

2. _____ Berlin

3. _____ Bear

4. _____ Bering Sea

5. _____ Bee

6. _____ Belgium

1. _____ Panda

2. _____ Pago Pago

3. _____ Panama Canal

4. _____ Painted Desert

5. _____ Pandora

6. _____ Papaya

> ■ Names in a telephone book are listed in alphabetical order, according to last names. When several people have the same last name, their names are arranged in alphabetical order, according to first names.   EXAMPLE: Barnes, John; Barnes, William; Barton, Clyde; Barwin, James D.

E. Copy the names in the order you would find them in a telephone book.

Donna Cameron _____

T. C. Caskey _____

James Callahan _____

Louis J. Caskey _____

Robert Kruse _____

Cindy Lyons _____

Paul Lyndale _____

Karen Krull _____

Dictionary: Guide Words

> ■ **Guide words** are words that appear at the top of each page in a dictionary. They show the first and last entry words on the page. Guide words tell whether an entry word is listed on that page. EXAMPLE: **beets/beyond:** The word <u>begin</u> will appear on the page. The word <u>bid</u> will not.

A. Read each pair of guide words and the list of entry words below. Put a check in front of each entry word that would appear on the page.

1. **blade/bluff**

_____ blur _____ blast

_____ blink _____ black

_____ blame _____ blaze

_____ blossom _____ blunder

_____ blush _____ blouse

2. **intend/island**

_____ into _____ invent

_____ instrument _____ isn't

_____ introduce _____ irrigate

_____ iron _____ itch

_____ inward _____ invite

B. Read each pair of guide words and the list of entry words below. Circle only the entry words that would appear on the page. Then write those words in the order in which they would appear in the dictionary.

1. **meal/minister**

meanwhile _____

melody _____

meadow _____

mention _____

mischief _____

2. **product/provide**

professor _____

propeller _____

proceed _____

program _____

protest _____

3. **rear/rescue**

recess _____

realize _____

recognize _____

reckon _____

receive _____

4. **miserable/mitten**

mist _____

mischief _____

miss _____

mite _____

mixture _____

Dictionary: Syllables

> - A **syllable** is each part of a word that is pronounced at one time.
> - Dictionary entry words are divided into syllables to show how to divide a word at the end of a writing line.
> - Put a **hyphen** (-) between syllables when dividing a word.
>   EXAMPLE: a-wak-en

- Find each word in a dictionary. Write the word, placing a hyphen between syllables.

1. chemical   chem-i-cal
2. gasoline _____
3. degree _____
4. marvelous _____
5. disappear _____
6. chimney _____
7. continent _____
8. miserable _____
9. generally _____
10. glacier _____
11. arithmetic _____
12. exercise _____
13. hospital _____
14. problem _____
15. window _____
16. language _____
17. agriculture _____
18. parakeet _____
19. beginning _____
20. simple _____

21. determine _____
22. musician _____
23. salary _____
24. cheetah _____
25. interrupt _____
26. dentist _____
27. recognize _____
28. rascal _____
29. innocent _____
30. educate _____
31. achievement _____
32. darling _____
33. homestead _____
34. calendar _____
35. missionary _____
36. farewell _____
37. aluminum _____
38. bacteria _____
39. program _____
40. banana _____

- Each dictionary entry word is followed by a respelling that shows how the word is **pronounced,** or said.
- **Accent marks** (′) show which syllables are said with the most stress.   EXAMPLE: au-to-mat-ic (ô′ tə mat′ ik)
- A **pronunciation key** (shown below) explains the other symbols used in the respelling.

A. Answer the questions below about the respelling of the word <u>automatic</u>. Use the pronunciation key at the right. (ô′ tə mat′ ik)

at; āpe; fär; câre; end; mē; it; īce; pîerce; hot; ōld; sông; fôrk; oil; out; up; ūse; rüle; pu̇ll; tûrn; chin; sing; shop; thin; <u>th</u>is; hw in white; zh in treasure. The symbol ə stands for the unstressed vowel sound in about, taken, pencil, lemon, and circus.

1. What is a key word for the symbol <u>ô</u>? _____

2. What is a key word for the symbol <u>ə</u>? _____

3. What is the key word for the symbol <u>a</u>? _____

4. What is the key word for the symbol <u>i</u>? _____

B. Use the pronunciation key as you look at each respelling. Underline the word for which the respelling stands.

1. (ə ban′ dən)   ability   abandon   aboard
2. (bak′ strōk′)   backstop   bakery   backstroke
3. (klench)   clef   clench   clerk
4. (dān′ tē)   daisy   dainty   dance
5. (hīt)   height   hit   hint
6. (en tīr′ lē)   entirely   entry   entertain
7. (wi<u>th</u>′ ər)   whether   withhold   wither
8. (noiz)   nosy   noise   nose
9. (ôt)   out   at   ought
10. (wāt)   wit   white   weight
11. (wâl)   wall   walk   wail
12. (vizh′ ən)   vision   visible   visit
13. (frāt)   free   fright   freight
14. (our)   hope   hour   ours
15. (dī′ mənd)   demand   diamond   dime
16. (sat′ əl īt′)   satisfy   salary   satellite
17. (mī′ grāt)   mighty   migrate   migrant
18. (ang′ gəl)   angry   angle   anger

> - A dictionary lists the **definitions** of each entry word. Many words have more than one definition. Sometimes a definition is followed by a sentence showing a use of the entry word.
> - A dictionary also tells the **part of speech** for each entry word. An abbreviation (shown below) stands for each part of speech.
>   EXAMPLE: **aunt** (ant, änt) *n.* **1.** the sister of one's father or mother. **2.** the wife of one's uncle.

A. Use the dictionary sample below to answer the questions.

au-di-ence (ô′ dē əns) *n.* **1.** a group of people gathered in a place to hear or see, such as those watching a movie at the theatre. **2.** an opportunity of being seen or heard; hearing: *He will explain as soon as he has an audience.* **3.** a formal meeting with someone of importance: *The committee will serve as your audience so that you can present your plan.* **4.** people who enjoy and support something: *Baseball has a large audience in America.*

au-di-o-vis-u-al (ô′ dē ō vizh′ ōō əl) *adj.* **1.** the type of materials that aid in teaching or learning through the use of both hearing and sight. **2.** of or relating to hearing and sight.

au-di-to-ri-um (ô′ də tôr′ ē əm) *n.* **1.** a large hall in a school, church, or other public building. **2.** a room or building used for large, public gatherings.

au-di-to-ry (ô′ də tôr′ ē) *adj.* of, relating to, or experienced through hearing.

1. How many definitions are given for the word

   audience? _____ for the words audiovisual and

   auditorium? _____ for the word auditory? _____

2. Which part of speech does the abbreviation n.

   stand for? _____

3. Which part of speech is audiovisual and

   auditory? _____

4. Which words in the dictionary sample are

   nouns? _____

n.	noun
pron.	pronoun
v.	verb
adj.	adjective
adv.	adverb
prep.	preposition

B. Write the number of the dictionary definition used for the underlined word.

1. _____ At the end of the movie, the audience clapped loudly to show how much they had enjoyed it.

2. _____ All the Olympic gold medal winners were given an audience with the President.

3. _____ The prisoner asked for an audience with the prison officials.

Review

A. Use the sample dictionary page below to answer the questions that follow.

traffic / transatlantic

traf-fic (traf′ ik) *n.* **1.** people, automobiles, ships or similar objects coming and going along a route or way of travel: *There was a lot of traffic at the ballpark after the game.* **2.** buying and selling, especially for profit; an exchange of goods. **3.** dealing in something improper or illegal: *Our government is trying to stop the drug traffic in our country.* **4.** the business done by a transportation system.

trail-blaz-er (trāl′ blā′ zər) *n.* **1.** a person who marks a trail to guide others; pathfinder. **2.** a pioneer: *She was a trailblazer in space exploration.*

train-ee (trā nē′) *n.* a person who is being trained for a job.

train-er (trā′ nər) *n.* **1.** one who trains. **2.** a machine or vehicle used in training. **3.** one who takes care of the minor injuries and is responsible for the physical training of an athlete, racehorse, or the like.

trai-tor (trā′ tər) *n.* **1.** one who betrays another's trust. **2.** one who practices treason.

tram-ple (tram′ pəl) *v.*, **tram-pled, tram-pling.** to stomp on; stamp with the foot; tread on so heavily as to crush or injure.

trance (trans) *n.* **1.** a condition somewhat like sleep, as that produced by hypnotism. **2.** a dreamy or stunned state: *He sat in a trance, dreaming of his summer vacation.*

tran-quil (trang′ kwəl) *adj.* calm; peaceful; free from disturbance. —**tran′ quil-ly, adv.**

trans-at-lan-tic (trans′ ət lan′ tik) *adj.* **1.** that which crosses or extends across the Atlantic Ocean: *They made a transatlantic telephone call.* **2.** on the other side of the Atlantic Ocean.

1. What are the guide words? _____

2. Which word has the most meanings? _____

3. Which words have only one meaning? _____

4. Which word is a verb? _____ How is its pronunciation shown? _____

5. Which words are nouns? _____

_____

6. Which word has the most syllables? _____

7. Which word has only one syllable? _____

8. Which words are adjectives? _____

9. Which word means "to stomp on"? _____

10. What is the meaning of tranquil? _____

_____

B. Write the number of the definition for the underlined word in each sentence.

1. _____ The Wright brothers were trailblazers in aviation.

2. _____ My brother is a trainer for the junior high football team.

3. _____ Friday evening traffic on the highway was heavy.

4. _____ I call my pen pal my transatlantic friend.

84   Unit 6, Study Skills

A. Learn the directions for Al's special recipe. Put the lines of the mixed-up poem in alphabetical order according to the first word or the first four letters of each line. Then read the poem in order.

1. _____ He finds instead a knife will do.

2. _____ But that is what Al hasn't got.

3. _____ Medium-sized glass bowl (his mom won't mind).

4. __1__ Al makes a most delicious snack,

5. _____ Whether Al cuts it thick or thin,

6. _____ Plus raisins (a half-cup of each will do).

7. _____ His pan is square, the eight-inch kind.

8. _____ (Ounces—eleven—quite a lot.)

9. _____ His mom cries, "Careful, that might cut you!"

10. _____ Stir then, Al, and spread in pan.

11. _____ As he uses kitchen bric-a-brac.

12. _____ You'll want him to invite you in.

13. _____ Pat it lightly with your hand.

14. _____ Peanuts next, and coconut, too.

15. _____ Beth's food grinder would help a lot.

16. _____ Now he chops some apricots,

B. Answer these questions about the poem.

1. What pan does Al need? _____

2. What ingredients are called for? _____

3. What does Al's mom want him to be careful with? _____

4. What quantity of raisins, coconut, and peanuts is needed? _____

   of apricots? _____

5. Once the recipe is done, what will you want Al to do? _____

C. Write the words below in alphabetical order on the lines opposite their respellings and definitions.

| caravan | academy | achievement | accompany |
| barter | anxious | decree | |

1. _____ (ə kad′ ə mē) **1.** a private high school. **2.** a school giving training in a special field.

2. _____ (ə kum′ pə nē) **1.** to go along with. **2.** to perform a musical accompaniment for.

3. _____ (ə chēv′ mənt) **1.** something achieved by unusual effort. **2.** the act of achieving.

4. _____ (angk′ shəs) **1.** uneasy, worried, and fearful. **2.** earnestly and eagerly desiring.

5. _____ (bär′ tər) **1.** to trade without using money. **2.** something bartered.

6. _____ (kar′ ə van′) **1.** a number of vehicles traveling together. **2.** a company of merchants going together for safety, especially across deserts.

7. _____ (di krē′) **1.** a decision or order issued by a court. **2.** any official decision or order.

D. Write a word from the list above that makes sense in the numbered blank. Then write the number of the definition used.

John was happy to graduate from the military <u>(1)</u> he had attended. He had worked hard to learn a lot about history. Because of John's record of <u>(2)</u> in history, he was invited to <u>(3)</u> his history teacher on a special trip to northern Africa. There they would travel with a <u>(4)</u> of Arab traders. They would watch the traders <u>(5)</u> with native tribes. They would obey any <u>(6)</u> of the tribe leaders. He was <u>(7)</u> to get started on the trip.

1. _____
2. _____
3. _____
4. _____
5. _____
6. _____
7. _____

Synonyms, Antonyms, and Homonyms ▪ Write S before each pair of synonyms. Write A before each pair of antonyms. Write H before each pair of homonyms.

1. _____ kind, cruel

2. _____ stop, halt

3. _____ been, bin

4. _____ together, apart

5. _____ come, arrive

6. _____ build, destroy

7. _____ beet, beat

8. _____ take, seize

9. _____ I'll, aisle

10. _____ help, hurt

11. _____ grow, increase

12. _____ here, there

13. _____ mane, main

14. _____ locate, find

15. _____ same, different

Prefixes and Suffixes ▪ Add a prefix or a suffix from the box to the underlined word in each sentence to form a new word that makes sense in the blank.

1. Mom was <u>happy</u> with her new lawn mower but became

_____ when it didn't work.

2. She <u>read</u> the directions again, thinking that she had

_____ them the first time.

3. Dad tried to _____ a loose <u>wire</u>.

4. When he couldn't <u>repair</u> it, he decided it was not

_____.

5. Our <u>good</u> neighbor showed her _____ by loaning
Mom her lawn mower.

```
-able
mis-
-ness
re-
un-
```

Contractions and Compound Words ▪ Write the two words that make up the contraction in each sentence. Then underline the compound word in each sentence. Draw a line between the two words that make up each compound word.

1. _____ _____ "Let's play baseball at recess," said Kim.

2. _____ _____ "I can't," said Bob. "My shoelace is broken."

3. _____ _____ "I'd like to be an outfielder," said Peg.

4. _____ _____ "You'll have to play underwater today," said
Justin. "It just started raining!"

Recognizing Sentences ▪ Write <u>S</u> before each sentence.

1. _____ Many interesting facts about bees.

2. _____ Bees have five eyes.

3. _____ On an ounce of honey for fuel.

4. _____ Bees tell other bees the distance to pollen areas.

Types of Sentences ▪ Identify the types of sentences below by writing <u>D</u> before a declarative sentence, <u>IN</u> before an interrogative sentence, <u>IM</u> before an imperative sentence, and <u>E</u> before an exclamatory sentence.

1. _____ Did you know that there are 20,000 kinds of bees?

2. _____ There is so much to learn about bees!

3. _____ Tell me how much honey each person in the United States eats each year.

4. _____ Honey producers say the average is about one pound per person.

Subjects and Predicates ▪ Draw a line between the subject and the predicate in each sentence below. Underline the simple subject once. Underline the simple predicate twice.

1. The honey-making industry makes $115 million each year.
2. An average bee can fly fifteen miles in an hour.
3. A worker honeybee makes less than one-eighth teaspoon of honey in its lifetime.
4. Its lifetime is just one growing season.
5. Two hundred bees make about one pound of honey in one season.

Run-on Sentences ▪ Separate the run-on sentences below. Write the last word of the first sentence. Place a period after the word. Then write the first word of the second sentence. Be sure to capitalize that word.

1. A waxy material is released by bees, it is used to make candles and polishes. _____

2. The robber flies kill bees, these flies have piercing beaks. _____

Singular, Plural, and Possessive Nouns ▪ Complete the chart below.
Write the forms called for in each column.

Singular Noun	Plural Noun	Singular Possessive	Plural Possessive
1. actor			
2. baby			
3. beach			
4. ox			
5. woman			
6. child			

Action Verbs and Linking Verbs ▪ Underline each verb or verb phrase in the sentences below.

1. The little Lion-Dog was once a palace guard dog in Tibet.
2. The Lion-Dog got its name because of the breed's thick, lion-like mane.
3. Today, Lhasa apso is the name of the breed.
4. Mainly a companion or a show dog, the Lhasa apso will guard its master's home.
5. Lhasa apsos gaze out a window at each passerby.

Using Verbs Correctly ▪ Circle the correct verb in parentheses.

1. Heather and Emily had (went, gone) to the pet store to get a dog.
2. They immediately (fell, fallen) in love with Bunny, a white puppy with black markings.
3. Bunny was (housebroke, housebroken) and would (sit, set) up and beg.
4. Heather and Emily had never (saw, seen) a friendlier dog.
5. "(Can, May) we buy her, Mom?" Heather asked.
6. "Yes," said Mom, "if you take (good, well) care of her."
7. "We'll (learn, teach) her some tricks, too," Emily said.

Capitalization ▪ Correct the student report below. Circle each letter that should be capitalized. Write the capital letter above it.

Last july mom and dad took my sister pam and me on a trip

to yellowstone national park. we drove through the grand

teton mountains in wyoming on the way. before we left home

we read a book named *the history of the old west* by

dr. e. j. james. i liked watching the geyser named old faithful.

it shoots water up over 115 feet every 65 minutes.

but my favorite stop was cody, wyoming. it was founded by

colonel william f. cody, known as buffalo bill.

Using Commas and End Punctuation ▪ Add commas and the correct end punctuation as needed in each sentence.

1. Yellowstone National Park was established in 1872
2. There are many hot springs in the park and wildlife is protected there
3. Moose deer antelope bear and other smaller animals are at home in the park
4. What a great variety of geysers can be seen there
5. You can enjoy canyons waterfalls lakes forests and meadows
6. Be sure to see Emerald Pool when you visit the park
7. Can you picture a hot spring colored by the blue sky
8. The Upper Falls of the Yellowstone River drop 109 feet and the Lower Falls drop 308 feet
9. What a beautiful sight the waterfall is
10. Yes Yellowstone Park is a national treasure

Using Commas and Quotation Marks ▪ Add commas and quotation marks as needed.

1. Have you heard of the Earthquake of 1959? asked a ranger.
2. Over eighty million tons of rock fell from the canyon wall and created a dam named Earthquake Lake he explained.

Topic Sentences ▪ Write a topic sentence for the paragraph below.

My dog and I play ball together. We go on hikes together. My dog is always happy to see me. My dog barks to let me know that a stranger is near. I can teach my dog to obey and to do tricks. I feed and bathe my dog.

TOPIC SENTENCE: _____

Clustering ▪ Complete the cluster by writing words that the topic in the center of the cluster makes you think of.

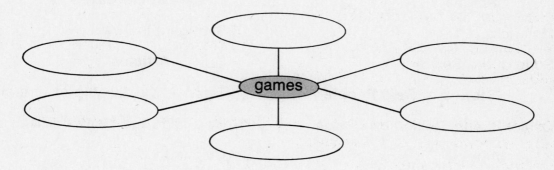

Audience ▪ Underline the audience named below to whom you would address a paragraph about games.

1. your classmates

2. your family

3. a company that manufactures games

Writing a Paragraph ▪ Now write a paragraph about games. Keep the audience you chose in mind. Write a topic sentence and four sentences that contain supporting details. The supporting details may be reasons, facts, or examples.

Games

_____

_____

_____

_____

_____

_____

Composition

Alphabetical Order ▪ Read the sample index of a reading book below.
Number the boldfaced titles of chapters in alphabetical order. Then
number the names of the selections in each chapter in alphabetical order.

INDEX: Types of Reading

_____ **Plays**

_____ Wizards Speak

_____ In School Daze

_____ **Poems**

_____ Limericks

_____ Song of the Semis

_____ **Stories of Real People**

_____ Daniel Boone, Wilderness Guide

_____ Young Abe

_____ **Fiction**

_____ Horses of Her Own

_____ Johnny Appleseed

_____ Mystery in the Cave

_____ Strangers in Town

_____ **Articles**

_____ Tigers in Captivity (a picture article)

_____ Be a Clown (a picture article)

_____ Cunning Coyotes

Guide Words ▪ Read the guide words for a dictionary page below. Put a
check before each entry word that would appear on that page.

1. eggnog / eject

_____ eggplant   _____ eight

_____ eel   _____ eggbeater

_____ either   _____ eject

_____ eggshell   _____ election

2. harbor / harp

_____ harm   _____ harp

_____ hare   _____ happy

_____ harvest   _____ harmony

_____ harness   _____ haste

Pronunciation ▪ Use the pronunciation key as you look at each respelling.
Underline the word that matches the respelling.

1. (sin′ dər)   sender   cinder   single

   (_____ n)   navy   notion   nation

   (_____ rm)   harp   happy

                           slash   slice

                           mineral   manner

at; āpe; fär; câre; end; mē; it;
īce; pîerce; hot; ōld; sông; fôrk;
oil; out; up; ūse; rüle; pu̇ll; tûrn;
chin; sing; shop; thin; this;
hw in white; zh in treasure.
The symbol ə stands for the
unstressed vowel sound in
about, taken, pencil, lemon,
and circus.